Second Wind

Turnaround Strategies for Business Revival

Suzanne Caplan

E͟P͟
Entrepreneur.
Press

Editorial Director: Jere Calmes
Cover Design: Beth Hanson-Winter
Composition: CWL Publishing Enterprises, www.cwlpub.com

© 2003 by Suzanne Caplan
All rights reserved.
Reproduction of any part of this work beyond that permitted by Section 107 or 108 of the 1976 United States Copyright Act without the express permission of the copyright owner is unlawful. Requests for permission or further information should be addressed to the Business Products Division, Entrepreneur Media, Inc.

This publication is designed to provide accurate and authoritative information in regard to the subject matter covered. It is sold with the understanding that the publisher is not engaged in rendering legal, accounting, or other professional services. If legal advice or other expert assistance is required, the services of a competent professional person should be sought.
—From a Declaration of Principles jointly adopted by a Committee of the American Bar Association and a Committee of Publishers and Associations

ISBN 1-891984-47-0

Printed in Canada

Contents

INTRODUCTION: Turn Your Business Around xi
    Dealing with Downturns xiii
    How Deep Is the Downturn? xiv
    When Will Conditions Improve? xv
    How Must Your Business Change to Return to Prosperity? xvi
    Change Is Always a Challenge xvi

SECTION I: *Analyze Your Company*

CHAPTER 1. Understanding Financial Information 3
    Are Accurate Records Really Important? 4
    Accounting Terms 101 6
    Other Basic Terms in Accounting 7

CHAPTER 2. Seven Signs of Trouble That Can Threaten a Business 9
    1. Little or No Revenue Growth 10
    2. Deteriorating Capital Base 11
    3. Equipment Failures That Threaten Productivity 11
    4. Poor Employee Morale 12
    5. Unpaid Taxes 13
    6. Failure or Closing of Major Customer 14
    7. New Technology Creating Pricing Pressure 14

CHAPTER 3. Nine Questions You Must Ask About Your Business 16
    1. Are You Solvent? 18
    2. Is There Still a Business 17
    3. Do You Have the Resources to Serve
       Your Customers as They Expect? 18

    4. Will You Be Able to Get Vendor
       Credit Again? 18
    5. Are There Legal Actions Pending? 18
    6. Are Your Taxes Current? 18
    7. Do You Still Have a Relationship with Your Banker? ...19
    8. Do You Have Enough Horses for the Race? 19
    9. Is There Any Fire Left in You? 19

CHAPTER 4. Get Ready for Change 21
    You Lead by Example 22
    Don't Point Fingers 22
    The Vision Thing 22

SECTION II. *First Steps to Stability*

CHAPTER 5. Harvest Cash—the Critical Element 27
    The Importance of Cash 28
    Step 1. Collect Receivables Diligently 29
    Step 2. Ask for a Down Payment on a Big Order 31
    Step 3. Slow Down or Renegotiate Your Payables 32
    Step 4. Draw on Lines of Credit 34
    Step 5. Identify and Sell Dead Inventory and
       Unneeded Equipment 35
    Step 6. Barter Instead of Buying 36
    How Your Business Affects Your Personal Life 37
    Get Control of Your Personal Cash Needs 38
    Be Cautious About Putting Personal Funds
       into the Business 39
    Use Your Cash to Stabilize Your Business and Yourself ...40

CHAPTER 6. Pull Back Major Projects for Review 41
    A Quick Fix Is Not the Answer 42
    A Company in Distress Can't Afford Another Mistake ...42
    Don't Take on New Business Just to Keep Busy 44
    You Can't Afford to Sell at a Loss for Long 46
    Freeze Hiring Plans 46
    Don't Send out Distress Signals—Create a Positive Spin ..47

CHAPTER 7. Cut Expenses Across the Board 50
    Reducing Costs 51
    Determine the Amount of Savings Required 51
    Don't Spare Any Sacred Cows 53
    Combine Jobs to Cut Wages 54

Ask Your Vendors for Their Cooperation .... .56
Cut Your Personal Expenses .... .58

CHAPTER 8. **Create a Support Team** .... .60
You Need Help .... .61
Meet with Your Accountant .... .62
How Lawyers Can Be Helpful During Tough Times ..... .63
Bring All Professionals Together for a Meeting .... .65
How Your Banker Can Help You .... .66
Your Key Employees Are a Good Resource .... .67
Your Friends Can Become Informal Advisors .... .68

CHAPTER 9. **Open Lines of Communication** .... .71
Getting Real .... .72
Tell Your Employees the Facts as You Know Them ...... .72
Talk to Creditors .... .74
Communicate with Customers .... .77
Talk with Family and Friends .... .78
Keep Your Spirits Up and Your Outlook Positive .... .80

SECTION III: *Create a Strategic Plan for Success*

CHAPTER 10. **Prepare a Comprehensive Financial Analysis** ... .85
The Main Issues of a Financial Analysis .... .86
Has Your Overall Sales Volume Decreased? .... .92
Are Your Gross Profit Margins Sufficient? .... .93
Is Your Overhead in Line with Revenues? .... .94
Is Your Current Debt Service Too High? .... .95
Determine What Needs to Be Changed
to Become Profitable Again .... .95

CHAPTER 11. **The Elements of a Plan** .... .97
Create a Plan: .... .98
1. Identify the Goals for Your Company .... .98
2. Establish Three Top Priorities to Meet Each Goal ..... .99
3. Decide How Long It Will Take to Complete
Your Program 100
4. List Each Step Involved in Carrying Out Your Plan .. 101
5. How to Schedule a Progress Review 102

CHAPTER 12. **A New Marketing Strategy** .... .104
The Basic Elements of Your Marketing Plan .... .105
1. Who Are Your Best Customers? 106

2. What Benefits Make Customers Choose
   Your Company? 107
3. Are There Additional Customers to Develop? 108
4. What Is the Best Way to Attract New Customers? 109
5. Is There a Cost-Effective Way to Market
   Your Company? 110
Project a Positive Image 111

CHAPTER 13. A Change in Overhead Expenses **113**
Review Each Line Item in Your Overhead Expenses 114
Determine the Value of Your Sales Expenses 115
Review Your Administrative Costs 117
Involve Your Managers in Overhead Review 117
Don't Create Unnecessarily High Stress 118
Some Costs Are Subject to Legal Constraints 119
Increase Productivity and You Will Increase Profit 119
Review All Your Debt 120
Questions to Consider in Reviewing Your Debt 121
Know Where You're Going Before You Begin 123

CHAPTER 14. A Look at Pricing Strategies **125**
Know Your Costs 126
Set Gross Profit Targets 126
Remember the Competition 127
Lower Prices = Higher Sales? 128
What About a Price Increase? 129
The Fallacy of the Million-Dollar Business 130

**CHAPTER 15. Create a Fallback Position—Crisis
               Management** **131**
Consider a Worst-Case Scenario 132
Learn the Basics About Bankruptcy 132
Examining Different Types of Bankruptcy 133
How a Chapter 11 Reorganization Can Help You 134
The Basics of Chapter 7 Bankruptcy 136
Other Options to Examine 137
Determine Whether Your Company Is Solvent 138
A Solvent Company Can Be Sold 140
Even an Insolvent Business Can Be Sold 141
Make a Plan in Advance—Always Good Advice 141
A Good Attorney Is Essential 142

CHAPTER 16. **Develop a Best-Case Scenario** 145
It's OK to Be Optimistic 146
Don't Cannibalize Inventory or Equipment
 to Raise Cash 146
Establish and Set New Goals 147
Create a Plan to Reach Your Goals 148
Share Your Optimism with Employees,
 Vendors, and Customers 148
Stay Aware of the Trends That Will
 Affect Your Company 149
Continue to Develop New Customers 150

SECTION IV: *Implement the Turnaround*

CHAPTER 17. **The Value of Outside Consultants** 155
Identifying the Problems 155
Setting Priorities and Developing a Strategy 156
Implementing the Plan 156
Finding Help at Universities 157
Getting Help from Public Agencies 158
Using Private Consultants 159
How to Choose a Good Consultant 160
How to Work Successfully with a Consultant 162

CHAPTER 18. **Employees—Options** 166
Keeping Key Employees 167
Consider Using Subcontractors 168
Part-Time Workers May Be Enough 169
Do You Know About Employee Leasing? 169
Hiring New Workers 170
Before Making the Offer 170
Take Time to Train 171

CHAPTER 19. **Renegotiating Terms on Loans and Leases** 173
How to Renegotiate Leases 174
Ask Your Landlord for Help 175
Do You Really Need to Own Your Building? 176
Rewrite Your Equipment Leases 177
What to Do About Auto Leases 178
How to Renegotiate Your Bank Debt 179
You Can Still Negotiate Delinquent Loans 180
How to Renegotiate with Your Vendors 181

CHAPTER 20. Gaining Profitability from Change **183**
    Develop an Operational Strategy for Change 184
    How to Analyze Your Profit on Products or Services 184
    Advertise, Market, and Sell for the Profits You Need 187
    How to Profit from Using a Subcontractor 188
    Sell an Unprofitable Line to a Competitor 189
    Liquidate Excess Inventory and Equipment 190
    Intangible Assets Have Tangible Value 192
    How to Continue Serving Customers While
        Terminating a Product or Service 193
    How to Promote What Your Business Does Well 194

**CHAPTER 21. Developing Controls to Keep the
                     Company on Track** **197**
    The Effective Operational Budget 198
    A Budget Must Be Flexible 199
    Creating an Organizational Chart 200
    Give Privileges and Expect Accountability 201
    Create Your Own Job Description 202

SECTION V: *Ensuring the Future*

CHAPTER 22. Establishing Benchmarks **207**
    What Growth Do You Expect? 208
    Where Will the Growth Come From? 208
    What Profitability Levels Are Your Goal? 209
    What New Technology Is Expected? 209
    Study What the Future Holds 210
    Can You Prepare Your Finances? 210
    Are There Ways to Leverage Growth? 211

**CHAPTER 23. Form New Partnerships and
                     Strategic Alliances** **213**
    What Is a Strategic Alliance? 214
    Some Reasons to Form Strategic Alliances 214
    Shared Resources 216
    Joint Product Development 216
    Virtual Corporations 217
    What to Look For in a Strategic Partner 217
    Consult with an Attorney 218
    Begin with a Confidentiality Agreement 219
    The Project Documents 219
    Creating an Operating Agreement 220
    A Word About Contracts 220

CHAPTER 24. Plan for Succession **222**
    Succession Must Be Based on Ability 223
    Succession Requires Managerial Talent 225
    The Succession Agreement 225
    Succession to an Unrelated Party 227

CHAPTER 25. Additional Exit Strategies—Mergers and Sales **229**
    Consider the Possibility of a Merger 230
    The Benefits of a Merger 231
    Finding a Merger Partner 233
    Getting Ready for a Sale or a Merger 233
    Once a Company Is in Play, the Environment Changes ..239

EPILOGUE: No Silver Bullets **240**

APPENDIX A. Bankruptcy **243**

APPENDIX B. Case Study: A Small Construction Company Stages a Comeback **246**

APPENDIX C. Advice from Professionals **255**

APPENDIX D. Glossary of Terms **268**

INDEX **279**

INTRODUCTION:
Turn Your Business Around

Business cycles are a fact of business life. There are not fixed rules about how long or how deep a downturn may be, just the fact that one will follow any period of growth. Products have a life cycle, as do entire industries. They can be precipitated by changes in taste or changes in technology. They can be global or regional. But they will be.

For example, after the high-tech-driven '90s dissolved into the dot-com fallout of 2001, recessionary forces were in place. It was the shock and loss of 9/11 that in a few short hours stopped sectors of the economy drastically. Airline business, along with hotels and restaurants, virtually ground to a halt. Sectors of the travel industry have changed forever.

For the business owner who has created a successful venture, the change of business conditions that threatens the ability of the company to thrive or even survive can be very scary. Day-to-day struggle becomes the first priority; understanding the dynamics of what is happening, much less creating a plan to return to stability, remains on the back burner. Here is a book to change that. It is a primer on how to turn around a business that is underperforming.

The strategy is not complex if you follow the steps outlined in these pages:

- Step One—Do an analysis of your current and recent financial performance.
- Step Two—Take steps to stabilize the operation.
- Step Three—Create a strategic plan before making any changes.
- Step Four—Implement the turnaround strategies.
- Step Five—Institute benchmarks and look to future possibilities.

You will begin with a serious look at where you've been and where you are currently. How weak is the company's financial position? In recent quarters, has it been deteriorating, stagnating, or even improving? If you have left the record keeping and the interpretation to others, such as your controller or CPA, now is the time you must change that. Finances are critical and clearly the responsibility of the owner/CEO.

Next, you must take steps to stop financial losses and change the environment of the company. You cannot afford the loss of support from any of your stakeholders, vendors, employees, or customers, so you must take steps to prevent this.

Even if you didn't start out with a written business plan, the time has come to create a formal strategic plan for change. It must be comprehensive and it must be in writing.

The fourth phase of a successful turnaround strategy is implementing your plan. How to change the company culture is an important element, which needs motivating leadership as well as a shared vision.

Finally, you must develop benchmarks that provide information on a timely basis on where the company is headed. Slight changes may indicate problems; the sooner you know, the quicker you can react. In addition, the need for future strategies, which may include strategic alliances or even mergers, will be a feature of this final turnaround phase.

No business or industry is exempt from change. Even among corporate giants with perceived financial strength, situations change that cause the need to make major adjustments in operations. General market conditions may soften. Interest rates may rise, choking off affordable capital or material. Energy costs may further shrink profit margins. All of these situations require attention: not to take action is to jeopardize the company's future.

The entrepreneur has a great challenge: even though your attention is almost consumed by the day-to-day operations, you must still look for signs of change—particularly those that affect the future success of your venture. And you want to take corrective steps as early as possible to prevent a nagging problem from turning into a disaster. This book will give you the guidelines for those steps.

Dealing with Downturns

Bill and Pat had known for months that something very serious was happening to their construction company. This was not the first time business was slow, but it was the first time that every payroll was a struggle and every check that was written involved a serious decision. Vendors were calling daily and the mail carried warnings of cancellations and potential lawsuits. It was every business owner's worst nightmare. It's a feeling I can understand: in the 21 years I was CEO of a small manufacturing company, I shared the experience.

I experienced my first recession a few years after I took over the family business, when the steel industry that was our major customer went through a major retraction. Massive layoffs and some plant closings were weekly events. We limped along at 50% of capacity for over a year until conditions improved. I did little to change. By the time another down cycle had begun, I had learned my lesson. Pain can be a powerful teacher.

As auto sales and construction starts were going down, I was preparing for its effect on steel production. We had diversified into other products and our production levels were manageable. No excess management or overhead costs were assumed. We were ready and, although we suffered (there is no way to avoid all difficulties), I felt far more in control of the fate of the company.

For the past decade, I have spent my time writing and speaking about entrepreneurship and consulting with small business clients throughout the United States. I have learned from working with a variety of industries that each has a rhythm and cycle unique to itself. And there are geographical differences as well. The dot-com disaster affected Northern California and the Pacific Northwest more than the Midwest. High unemployment rates in an area will impact all business: people have fewer dollars to spend on houses, clothing, or entertainment. But most important, perhaps, is that when market conditions soften and profits are squeezed, action must be taken. Sometimes the changes are slow and subtle and sometimes gut-wrenching, such as an unexpected global event or the bankruptcy or closing of a major customer. Ignoring the signs or denying the reality is inviting disaster. So the first part of my mission in this book is to make you aware of how to read the signs of trouble in your own business.

There are a number of questions you need to ask yourself once you determine that your company is going to be sailing through some rough waters—the sooner, the better.

How Deep Is the Downturn?

The information you need will come from news sources,

industry data, and direct customer inquiry. Do your homework and ask questions; what you will find out is critical to your own future. You need to keep your own operation in step with the demands of your clients/customers.

Business cycles are uneven: some sectors and some areas get hit harder than others. For the past two decades, the basic industry and manufacturing sector has shrunk dramatically. There have been major consolidations, followed by stable periods with some growth and then another downward cycle.

Until 2001, the tech sector saw little of these wild swings. But once the hardware industry reached saturation—most of those wanting computers or cell phones had them—the euphoria of rapid growth was over. Then the bottom fell out of the dot-com world and the signs are in place that future growth will be far slower.

Retailing and other service businesses will follow general economic trends. If this is your area, you are likely to be driven by current confidence and spending trends. The biggest problem you may face is a squeeze on profits.

When Will Conditions Improve?

Just as good times do not last forever, neither do difficult times. You may feel you are in a free fall, but you aren't. There will be a bottom: once you're there, circumstances will inevitably improve. When? Again, the source of the information is the general economic predictions, along with industry data and customer information.

The automotive industry knows the average age of the cars currently on the road and can predict when a replacement cycle will likely begin. Construction jobs ready to begin may affect your business level, as may inventory levels on the shelves of manufacturers or major retailers.

Whether you are cutting staff or restructuring debt, timing is an important element. Study the signs and work on interpreting what they mean to you.

How Must Your Business Change to Return to Prosperity?

Times change, people change, and products and services change. The business you started or have been operating is unlikely to look the same year after year. It may be the way you do things or it may even be what you do. Ten years ago, few companies sold products on the Internet; now most have at least a presence on the Web. People still buy books, but now the vast majority buy them in mega chains as well as on the Internet. The product is the same, but the delivery system has been altered.

And in this case, it is likely to change even further. Downloading books (as well as all other written material) into small, hand-held devices is on its way. Bottom line: the business is there; it just doesn't look at all like it did 20 years ago.

Change Is Always a Challenge

Even if you overhaul your product line, your delivery system, or your marketing strategy, there will be change coming. Some companies can make marginal changes and see improvements. Others will have to take fairly bold steps.

Even though the vision and the decision are yours, it won't be without some trepidation. Remember also that your employees and associates (including suppliers, vendors, and even customers) are concerned as well. Give them as much information as you can and keep them motivated. A larger part of your success will depend on execution and that will require more than just you.

SECTION I

▲ ▲ ▲

ANALYZE YOUR COMPANY

CHAPTER 1

UNDERSTANDING FINANCIAL INFORMATION

WHAT DO ALL THE NUMBERS MEAN?

> **D**on operated a sign company that grew from a small shop doing work for local retail companies to a million dollar firm doing highway signage. He wasn't afraid of hard work, coming in early in the morning to set up jobs in the shop and meeting with customers whenever they were available. Sales and operations were his strength, finance was not.
>
> As a small company with revenues under $120,000 annually, Don was able to pay his bills and take a reasonable salary. He thought that if he grew the business to a million dollars, he would be on easy street. Just the opposite occurred. More employees meant a bigger payroll, more equipment, and more raw materials. He felt as if more money was going out than coming in but wasn't sure why or what to do about it. Buying on credit perhaps?
>
> After the growing pressure and missed paychecks became too much, Don decided he'd better learn the financial mechanics of his own company. It was almost too late—low pricing and unexpected costs had created large losses and securing enough cash to keep operating was a real problem. Learning what to look for was Don's first step in a turnaround.

John is a master of artful printing, Mickey is a skilled contractor, and Debbie could sell anything to anyone at almost any time. They are all hard workers, intelligent, and well motivated and yet all three have gone through difficult times in their businesses. In one case, the cause was overexpansion; for another, a general slowdown of the economy had a serious effect; and the third had severe outside competitive pressures that dropped prices and profitability. But all three had one thing in common: none of them understood or, for that matter, really liked the financial side of business. And it is likely that the first element was a primary reason for the second: not understanding finances made them uncomfortable and that feeling is what they didn't like. Once the mystery behind the numbers is removed, they become far more interesting.

The financial management of a business is absolutely critical to its success. Of course, your company must produce a product or service that pleases your customer and customers must be found and convinced to make the decision to buy. The first comes under operations (which includes managing people and resources) and the second is under the general area of sales. The third leg of any business operation is finance, which involves setting prices and controlling costs and collecting money.

You do not need to be the one to keep the records; a bookkeeper or controller may be hired to manage that aspect. But you do need to review and understand the reports that are generated and make decisions based on what you discover.

Are Accurate Records Really Important?

When your company was new, you may have kept your own books by simply recording all cash revenue in a jour-

> *All companies should generate monthly profit and loss statements that are reviewed by management. Quarterly, these should be reviewed by an accountant as well.*

nal and using a checkbook to record expenses. At the end of the year, you took everything to an accountant, who produced a tax return. This works for a while, unless you are selected for a tax audit and need to produce receipts, etc. So, most of us understand that we must have records to prove how much we owe (or do not owe) in taxes. Yet, the greater the understanding, the more tax planning you can do—a very good reason to learn.

What you should also have learned along the way is that the accurate interpretation of how the business is doing also relies on accurate record keeping. All numbers must be put in their proper place so the strengths and the weaknesses of the company are evident. Paying personal expenses with a company check may be possible, but it will lower profits and give you a false picture of how the company is performing. If you do it, at least record it in a way you understand.

You may no longer be the one who keeps the checkbook or, more likely, maintains the data entry in the computer, but you must check from time to time to prevent errors. You will need basic accounting knowledge to do this.

And don't think it is purely the job of your accountant who prepares tax returns or interim profit and loss statements. By the time statements are done and you have met, too much time may have elapsed for you to have taken corrective action that prevents any further problems. The sooner you spot trouble, the sooner you can correct it.

For example, if your costs have gone up and lowered your profits, the speed with which you can either raise selling prices or lower controllable costs is critical. You need to be on alert in days, not months.

Accounting Terms 101

The first step is to know what basis your accounting system is on. The two choices are *cash* or *accrual*.

Most businesses use accrual basis accounting because, with only a few exceptions, the reports you generate will give you a more accurate view of how the company is doing. One of the exceptions to this may be a service business that deals mostly in cash, such as a restaurant. Customers pay by cash or credit cards, payments that turn into cash in a matter of days. The primary expenses are wages, which are paid on a timely basis, as well as the cost of food and beverage, which may often be paid on delivery. With few exceptions, most revenue and expense are realized in the same month.

No doubt a cash basis system is easier to set up and maintain. But if you make a large sale on credit or incur a large expense you do not pay for, you will not see this on a monthly statement. Therefore, you want to make the effort to establish and utilize an accrual system.

With the off-the-shelf accounting systems available, this is not that difficult. The two most widely used are QuickBooks and Peachtree; both are accrual systems as long as the data entry is made on a timely basis.

> *The two most popular off-the-shelf accounting software packages are QuickBooks (Quicken) and Peachtree Accounting. Both are menu-driven and user-friendly and produce income statements and balance sheets that are easy to generate and understand.*

Cash and Accrual

Cash basis means that you show income when money is actually received. A credit sale will show up only when the cash comes in. On the other side, expenses are shown only when they are paid, not when they are incurred.

Accrual basis refers to the system that recognizes income as soon as it is earned, whether it is received or not, and expenses at the time they are incurred, whether they are paid or not. All obligations, including taxes, will be accounted for.

Other Basic Terms in Accounting

We will be talking at length about profitability because this is the most critical consideration in returning to full financial health and remaining there. The main elements involved are setting and keeping an adequate pricing structure and controlling costs. Pricing is based on recovering your direct costs—those that are directly related to the purchase or production of your product or the labor and material cost of your service.

In a retail operation, the primary direct costs are for the goods and may also include inbound freight. In a service business, the direct costs are primarily labor. As an example, a restaurant will describe the cost of food and non-administrative labor as *direct* costs.

While these costs will go up or down depending on volume, their percentage of sales should remain the same. This means if you spend 60% of every revenue dollar on direct costs when your volume is 500,000, when it goes to one million, these costs should still be around 60%.

The other critical aspect of your operation that is found on your profit and loss statement is your fixed costs—your overhead. You incur these costs regardless of how high (or low) your revenue goes. Learning how to control these

Direct Costs

Direct (variable) costs, simply put, are those directly involved in producing or providing your goods or services. For example, if you are a manufacturer, the material and labor used to produce your product are direct costs. Those costs that are not related to the actual manufacturing are not.

These direct costs are also described as variable, because they go up or down according to the volume you are producing or selling. The more items you manufacture or sell, the more costs you will have.

Fixed Costs

Fixed (indirect) costs are involved with keeping the business open and operating, such as rent, utilities and administrative salaries. They are not directly connected to your product or service. They are considered fixed because they seldom vary, regardless of your volume of revenue. For example, if your rent is $2,000/month, it will remain the same whether your sales are $500,000 or one million.

costs is critical at all times, but particularly during slow times. Lowering your overhead costs lowers your break-even number—the volume at which you can begin making a profit.

You may be more comfortable just trying to increase sales or manage production, but unless you have the basic financial knowledge, you won't be able to set pricing goals that add to profits or to set budgets to manage overhead costs. These items are critical to any recovery.

Chapter Key Points

- Make sure records are accurate.
- Use one of the "off the shelf" accounting systems to get numbers in "real time."
- An accrual system is likely to give a more accurate picture.
- Learn to read an Income Statement, not just glance at it.

CHAPTER 2

SEVEN SIGNS OF TROUBLE THAT CAN THREATEN A BUSINESS

KNOW THE SYMPTOMS

> *Keith knew his company was struggling, but he wasn't sure how serious it had become. The 20-year-old construction company that he started had grown for many years but had stagnated over the past three. Sales were flat but the cost of insurance and wages continued to increase, evaporating all profits and using up all his working capital.*
>
> *Old trucks needed to be replaced, but he had no cash to spend and, virtually all of the time, equipment sat idle because it wasn't working. Materials weren't available when needed because the company's credit was poor.*
>
> *Many of the employees had been with the company a long time and they had a good personal relationship with Keith. Even though, morale was deteriorating and productivity suffered. All of the signs that the future of the enterprise was in jeopardy were there—Keith didn't want to see them.*

Understanding more about the financial performance of your company will help you see trends as they are developing and not wait until a crisis. Some problems are acute—they happen suddenly—and some are chronic—they go on for years and you learn to live with them. Here are seven situations that should put up red flags.

1. Little or No Revenue Growth

Early-stage companies normally experience substantial growth as customers find you and your market enthusiastically. Then there is a leveling-off period when growth seems to slow and then stop. It may work to spend a short period at that plateau while you allow your business systems to grow to handle the volume. But then you must look at ways to get back on the growth path.

The reasons not to do so are understandable. You may be working 50-60 hours a week just to handle what you have and there is little time to find new clients, even if you thought you could handle their business. But growth is a necessity—because even with a reasonable level of inflation, flat revenues really mean a loss of revenues in terms of real dollars.

And, as you know, the costs to operate your business *never* go down. Rent, utilities, phone, and even postage are always going up. And wages too, including your own. As your employees become more experienced, you will want to pay them commensurate with their contributions, so raises are understandable, in benefits as well as salary. You may have added insurance and additional vacation time. All of this has a cost. And you need to replace and update equipment as well.

So what effect does flat growth have with this scenario? It lowers your profit. Costs become a greater percentage of revenue and ultimately profits become smaller. It may begin to create a serious cash squeeze and imperil your ability to pay debts and keep up with needed equipment purchases or repair.

2. Deteriorating Capital Base

Periods of flat growth in revenue can cause a negative cash flow. You need a steady stream of profit to allow cash to pay principal debt service and allow for reinvestment in new technology, equipment, or new project development.

After a fairly short time, you will find yourself in a double bind. You aren't generating enough cash to fund any meaningful growth and this lack of profits may prevent you from borrowing to fund it as well.

If you have gotten to this point, chances are your alternatives are few. One may be to look to outside investors for funds, although you may have to give up a good bit of control to get the capital you need. The other possibility is to sell off assets to raise cash. This may be a dangerous strategy, without considerable thought. You don't want to sell something you will need later on. Selling slow-moving inventory at a loss will affect profits as well as solvency.

3. Equipment Failures That Threaten Productivity

Not having positive cash flow will not just jeopardize growth; it will also affect current operations. If your equipment is not operating properly, your production may be slower, or quality not what you need or expect. In addition, total breakdowns will stop production and cause employees to stand around not accomplishing any work. This will raise your direct costs and lower profits even further.

> **Profit** is the excess of revenue over expense. **Cash flow** represents the available cash to pay current expenses.

> *Tip* — Advice from banker Tom Nunnally: "It is never a good idea to borrow from an unwilling participant such as vendors or taxing bodies."

Perhaps more important, if you miss delivery dates and disappoint customers, you may lose some business, further lowering revenue. You can begin a downhill spiral as a result.

4. Poor Employee Morale

Look around at your employees and give close consideration to what you see. Are they angry, disillusioned, or confused? Are they short of inventory; working on substandard equipment, or always fending off threatening phone calls? Are you communicating with them?

Surely you know that having good employees is a contributing factor in the growth and success of your venture. So it makes sense that when (and if) they feel negative, this will have the opposite effect. The most immediate result will be diminished productivity. People who don't care, show it. They take more time off and seldom think of ways to accomplish the task at hand more quickly or more efficiently. If wages are frozen or bonuses missed, the attitude becomes "What's the use?" And your job becomes tougher because the need to communicate becomes more urgent. We will cover this topic completely, later in this book.

And remember as well, your employees are often the public face of your company. If they have gripes, that's where they may air them. I still remember traveling on TWA Airlines in the midst of its most difficult times. All you heard from employees were complaints and dissatisfaction. It made the trip uncomfortable and forced me, a fairly frequent flyer, to look at other airlines. I wasn't the only one, and the loss of business further hurt the weakened airline.

There are not merely business reasons to care about the concerns of workers. There are human reasons as well and you want to keep a sense of community in your company.

> *The aggressive new companies that are hungry for new business are looking for your dissatisfied customers.*

5. Unpaid Taxes

No business owner sets out to get into trouble with the tax collector. Most of us have enough sense to know how painful that can be. But it may start accidentally and grow quickly. It often starts with a single payroll when the money isn't fully available. Pay checks are issued with the expectation that withheld taxes will be covered as soon as customers begin to pay outstanding invoices. But by the time these payments are received, other bills have to be paid or another payroll is coming up. Before you know it, taxes are owed and the money just isn't there. Now you are on dangerous territory.

First of all, many taxing bodies have the power to collect that exceeds those of ordinary creditors. They can make a demand for payment, file a lien, and execute a levy on your bank or even your customers in record time. They are effective collectors.

Second, the financial burden grows very quickly, particularly if unpaid returns are not filed. For federal taxes, there are penalties both for failure to file and for failure to pay—5% per *month*. So, in the end, you won't just be paying the tax, you will be paying back the tax plus penalty and interest.

Another consideration is the possibility of personal liability. If you are the responsible officer, that is, the one who makes the financial decisions, an assessment can be made against you as well as your company. Then the collection actions will be aimed at your assets.

And if all this weren't enough to motivate, there is also the matter of criminal prosecution. It is unlikely for payroll taxes, but it is far more frequent for not remitting sales tax. That is often charged as theft, as the money belongs to the state, not your company.

> *This is the place you work too and the environment will affect your performance as well as that of your employees.*

> **Tip** The IRS penalties are steep: 5% per month for failure to pay tax and 5% per month for failure to file returns.

If your business has found itself in this kind of trouble, see a professional as soon as you can. This is one problem you can't ignore!

6. Failure or Closing of Major Customer

Most new businesses are warned about becoming dependent on a single customer or even a few. That is easy in theory, but often difficult in practice. When a customer offers you a lot of business, it isn't easy to turn it down. If you are in an industry where there are only a few players of any size, this may be your reality.

If it is and one of these major customers cuts back operations, files for reorganization, or closes, your entire business may be jeopardized. So pay attention to what is happening within the industry as well as with your customers.

If payments get slower, take some action. If the company is big enough, the accounting side does not talk to the purchasing side, so you won't lose the business. Anyway, if you're not going to get paid, you don't want the sale. I had a client who was a small electrical contractor who allowed a major *Fortune* 100 company to get so far behind that my client had to file bankruptcy. Minimize your exposure.

If orders slow down, don't wait until they stop: get out and look for new business. At the same time, keep your lines of communication up with your customer. These are the times when you have to work hard just to stay even.

7. New Technology Creating Pricing Pressure

The landscape of America is full of rusted plants, some of which are still partially in operation. It's impossible to believe that they could be efficient. Jobs that were done by workers are now being done by robots. Planning production is done by computer. Inventory and shipping are managed by scanners. The years bring new technology: if older companies cannot afford to keep up, they are likely unable to compete.

Labor-intensive businesses must be able to avail themselves of labor-saving devices. Pricing pressures come from those domestic companies that can afford to do so in addition to the offshore operations that use low-cost labor. Staying in business without making a profit makes little sense.

These are not the only serious problems a company can run into. I could write a book about the perils of the dot-com companies, their overuse of venture capital and underuse of business models. Regardless how new an idea is and how clever the folks who thought it up, business is now and will always be about revenue exceeding costs and creating profit. This is not a theory; it is a reality and you must have a stream of income.

The latest and greatest idea may come and go, but at the end of the day, it's hard work and good dealings that secure the future for most businesses.

> *The basic measure of a business is the return on owner's equity. Are you making money on your investment or would it return more somewhere else?*

Chapter Key Points

- Companies need growth to cover overhead cost increases.
- Working capital is critical to stability.
- Productivity needs to be maintained by technology as well as motivation.
- Unpaid taxes can grow quickly to disastrous levels.

CHAPTER 3

NINE QUESTIONS YOU MUST ASK ABOUT YOUR BUSINESS

DARE TO DIG FOR ANSWERS

Business owners begin to sense the rhythm of their own company—when trouble happens, they know even if they temporarily aren't willing to admit it to themselves.

Collections calls increase; payrolls are harder to cover; you spend much of your time looking for material you don't have to purchase COD. Customers complain and employees aren't happy and you spend less time planning the next moves and more time worrying about the last ones. If that is where you are, the time has come to sit down and consider your realities. Even if you don't think you'll like the answers.

Just as there are a number of different problems that a company can face, there are degrees of trouble, as well. Your first task is to decide if the condition of your business is mildly disturbing or whether it is critically imperiled. If cash flow has begun to get short and collections calls are being received, that can be disturbing and a bad sign but not critical unless it isn't handled and it goes on for a long time. So now is the time to ask yourself exactly how you are doing and think over those answers. A true entrepreneur is an optimist but that doesn't mean you can ignore reality in the hopes that it will right itself. It seldom will.

1. Are You Solvent?

Simply put, do your debts exceed your assets? If they do, it is a cause for concern. But even if they don't, there are some signs you should look for, namely how your current assets and liabilities match up—*liquidity*. Current assets include cash, accounts receivable, and current inventory. Current liabilities include accounts payable and current loan payments.

Liquidity measures your ability to retire obligations due over the short term by available cash or expected receipts. If all of your assets are invested in a building and all of your debt is short term to vendors, you are in a cash crunch. The only way out is to sell the property to get the cash or file for Chapter 11 bankruptcy to turn current debt into long-term debt. It's time to consult an attorney.

2. Is There Still a Business?

No one shoes horses anymore and we all know that. But there are other businesses that have gone away and the realization doesn't sink in for years. The steel industry is one: there is a market for low-priced imports, but hardly one for domestically produced goods. Giant bookstores have threatened the life of the independent bookseller. Travel agencies are being damaged by online services and online airline sites and decreasing commissions. Take a hard look at your business—is there still a demand for you to provide your goods or services at a fair price and a profit? If not, can you change and meet a new demand?

You may have to face the fact that the life cycle for your business is over and, before you go deeper into debt, it may be time to close. Or you may be able to sell to someone who can take it in another direction.

> ***Liquidity*** *is determined by comparing the total current assets to the total current liabilities. The ratios vary by industry, but the trends are critical.*

> **Tip** — A mature product line may have value to other companies as they have existing customers as well as new ones who will purchase additional products from them.

3. Do You Have the Resources to Serve Your Customers as They Expect?

When a company gets into some difficulty, one of the early signs is lower inventory and delayed shipments. If you are manufacturing, chances are you are not able to produce without sufficient raw materials. If you sell products, you may be losing sales because you don't have what your customers want, when they want it.

If you are spending too much of your day listening to pleas and complaints about your delivery/service to customers, pay attention—the handwriting is on the wall.

4. Will You Be Able to Get Vendor Credit Again?

You can survive without vendor credit over the short term but it is almost impossible to run a cash-out business unless you do most of your business in cash. If your vendors are angry enough that they won't trust you again, you have a critical problem. If that hasn't happened yet, make sure it doesn't.

5. Are There Legal Actions Pending?

Be honest. Are there unopened letters in your drawer from lawyers or the court, warning you about legal action from collections? Are you having your company lawyer stall the inevitable, that you will lose as soon as your latest bluff is over? If so, now you are spending money for attorneys while still being in debt. A bad sign—pay attention.

6. Are Your Taxes Current?

In Chapter 2 I discussed in length the importance of taxes.

If this is the only one of these eight questions that you answer negatively, you can probably figure out a way to structure a payment plan. But if it is one of a number of problems you identify, you are on the critical list.

7. Do You Still Have a Relationship with Your Banker?

Have you missed interest payments and left phone calls unreturned? Do you avoid going to the bank to transact business because you don't want to run into your banker, who used to be a good friend? If you are going to successfully complete a turnaround, you will need a good bank that will try to help. Now may be the time to find a second bank and start off on the right foot.

> *Regardless of the tone of any collection letter, a creditor cannot just walk into your business and take what is owed. There is a legal procedure that may take months to complete.*

8. Do You Have Enough Horses for the Race?

Have your better employees already left to seek their fortune somewhere else? Are others looking because they are working part time, holding uncashed paychecks to help out in a cash crunch or have little faith in the company's future? You remember how long it takes to find good workers and how long it takes to train them and get them up to speed. If you can, try to do what it takes to hold on to the ones you have now.

9. Is There Any Fire Left in You?

A turnaround is a challenging task. It's a good thing that most entrepreneurs welcome a challenge! But do not take what is in front of you too lightly. Seriously ask yourself if you have the energy and desire to commit the time and effort that is needed. This may even be more difficult than starting a new company. If you aren't sure, we have alternative suggestions in later chapters.

Reading through this first section is taking the first step—acknowledging that your company has problems that will not go away. Next we will begin to develop a plan to pinpoint the issues and take corrective action.

Chapter Key Points

- Analyze your ability to pay bills.
- Losing customers because of poor product selection or poor service is always hard to reverse.
- It takes resources to make a comeback.
- You're the leader and that requires conviction as well as energy.

CHAPTER 4

GET READY FOR CHANGE

FACE YOUR FEARS

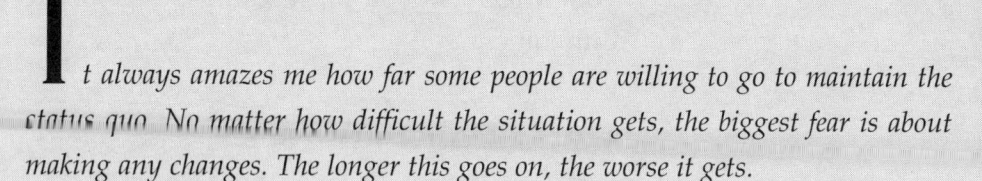

It always amazes me how far some people are willing to go to maintain the status quo. No matter how difficult the situation gets, the biggest fear is about making any changes. The longer this goes on, the worse it gets.

That is why I have spent several chapters describing some of the problems you may be having. Most business owners get to know the rhythm of their companies. When yours hits a sour note, you know. You see the signs of trouble and, if you don't take action, it will only get worse.

Let me give you the good news—there are a number of ways to deal with the problems of any business venture. We will discuss a step-by-step plan that will give you a road map to accomplish this—no magic bullet, but the chance to work hard with a purpose.

And now is the time for real leadership. Companies in trouble often have far too little of this. I have described this phenomenon as a "bus out of control without a driver" and received a knowing look from clients and particularly their employees. Does this sound familiar to you? Have you been hiding in your office, taking few phone calls and being very defensive about everything? It's understandable: the problems swirling around you seem overwhelming at times and you're not exactly sure what to do. So you do nothing, because that seems the safest.

Now is the time to take action—but not just any action. Well thought out and well planned action is required. It starts with you taking control. If you have been keeping a low profile, this is the time you must change that dramatically.

You Lead by Example

The very first thing you must do is step up, take charge, and face all of the problems head on. You are not responsible for all the mistakes: some of what happened is due to circumstances beyond your control. And your staff may have made their own share of mistakes. But it happened on your watch, so you must lead the organization out of its difficulties.

Don't Point Fingers

It doesn't matter if there is one person or circumstance that was the main cause of your problem—a customer that didn't pay his or her bill or a supplier that cut you off or a bank that canceled your line of credit. You don't have the time and energy to take them on and it's unlikely you could change the situation very much. Spend a day being angry, get it out of your system, and move on.

The Vision Thing

You must know where you are going if you ever expect to get there. You know what goals you had when you began and how you moved toward achieving them. Now you must redesign those goals and move the entire organization in that direction.

You will need to lead with energy and commitment and the ability to share the vision with others around you. Your ability to communicate, honestly and simply, is a critical element here. If you describe an action that seems reasonable, even if it is a bit ambitious, others will begin to believe that it is possible and their energy will grow as well.

Everyone will have to work together in order to turn around a company that is headed in the wrong direction. That movement starts with you.

You may have built a business where others thought it was impossible, so why can't you fix it even when the odds are not in your favor?

Change isn't easy—it requires great effort and a certain amount of risk. But the satisfaction of achievement is great when you've restored something worth saving.

Chapter Key Points

- Change happens first in those who lead.
- Others must share the belief that good things are likely to happen.
- You have to have a goal in mind and not drift aimlessly.

SECTION II

▲ ▲ ▲

FIRST STEPS TO STABILITY

HARVEST CASH—THE CRITICAL ELEMENT

GROW WITH THE FLOW

Acme Printing was a small offset printing company before they expanded in 2000 by purchasing a large and expensive five-color press. Their customer base increased as did the size of their receivables, their vendor credit and their debt service. This is a typical result of any growth spurt.

When sales flattened, the owner expected balance to return but it did not. Working capital remained low and problems increased. He considered lending his own funds to ease the stress. But, in the end, we convinced him to put another plan in place.

First, the company put an aggressive collection policy into action. Some large companies intend to stretch out payables and will do so unless a serious demand is placed on them. Others may institute a complicated paperwork trail that slows the procedure. You need to know their rules and assure that you've done the work necessary to be paid timely.

Acme made this a priority and that made a difference. On the payable side, they made longer term agreements with their vendors.

And finally, an older press was sold which allowed for some cash cushion. The combination of these actions brought in enough additional capital to allow for further analysis and other changes to make a long-term difference.

The Importance of Cash

Many business owners may not be able to analytically describe the difference between cash flow and profits, yet they know that both are required for long-term success. Eroding profits may take a long time to cause a problem for a company, but a sudden decrease in cash flow will cause immediate discomfort. On the other hand, sufficient cash flow may unfortunately mask potentially serious distress.

Restaurants are a good example of this. They may be losing thousands of dollars as a result of excessive owner's draw or uncontrolled shrinkage and these losses will be funded by growing debt. But they are collecting cash daily and, as long as there is cash to pay the most pressing bills, they can keep most creditors at bay.

Whenever a serious downturn occurs in any sector of the economy, it can be more life-threatening to small businesses than to larger corporations. A sudden drop in cash is a nightmare to most entrepreneurs. They aren't able to issue new stock and their loan sources dry up as well.

It makes sense, then, to create a cash cushion as the first step of any turnaround. You need to do it for solid business reasons as well as personal ones. From the perspective of your company, if you have funds available, you can make at least partial payments to satisfy vendors, cover an upcoming payroll, or keep your bank from getting wind of your problems and taking actions to make them worse.

From a personal perspective, your business situation is likely to create stress in your life that may be overwhelming at times. Having the cash to deal with at least some of the issues will make things easier for you. It's almost impossible to have a clear head to make decisions and exercise strong leadership if you have to spend your time selling personal assets or borrowing from friends to pay

> ## Six Steps to Increase Cash Flow
>
> 1. Increase collection activity.
> 2. Solicit advances on big jobs.
> 3. Slow down payables.
> 4. Draw on credit lines.
> 5. Sell excess inventory.
> 6. Decrease expenses using barter instead of cash payments.

employees or vendors that are threatening to shut you off. If you reduce this immediate roadblock, you can spend your time on critical analysis and keeping the ship afloat to sail again.

Now let's look at the six steps for increasing your cash flow.

Step 1. Collect Receivables Diligently

Many small business owners are the chief salespersons of their operation and over the years they develop personal relationships with their customers. These friendships can make an owner less likely to enforce tough collection policies: calling a friend for money isn't easy. If this is the way your company operates, you probably do little of the collection calling yourself. But someone must make these calls and it is absolutely necessary that you assign this task to someone in your organization, that you make sure that it is being done regularly, and that you require that reports be given to you. If this isn't the case currently, get your bookkeeper or controller on the job immediately.

If you are in a cash crunch, the same may also be true for your customers, but that doesn't mean they shouldn't be reminded about what they owe. If no one ever asks, you may never get paid, and that could be disastrous for your business. At some point, what may be required is a friend-

> *One of my customers told me that the only way he would ever pay me is if I would call. He said if I didn't care enough, neither did he. I've always remembered that..*

ly call from you to bring at least a partial payment, which could well be critical at this time.

You should develop procedures that become automatic once they are in place. At the end of each month, statements should be sent to all customers showing their outstanding balances. When a bill becomes 45 days old, a friendly written reminder is appropriate. After 60 days, a call is in order. After 90 days, it's time to take real action. I know that there are concerns about losing a customer, but you really must ask yourself if you want to do business with a company that isn't willing to pay its bills. Why not just give them product or service for free and save the administrative cost?

Offering discount terms may speed up cash flow. Although a 2% discount will affect your bottom line, this may be a viable short-term program to ease the financial squeeze. If profits have been an ongoing problem for your business, you need to be careful about which of your customers you offer this program to and how long you keep it in effect. You may find that you have some customers that take the 2% and still don't pay within the five- or 10-day period you require. If this happens, bill them for the unearned discount and cancel the program.

Establish a Successful Collection Program

To enact a well-managed collection program, do the following:
- Check references before granting credit.
- Always establish terms in writing.
- Send regular statements.
- Make calls on past due accounts.
- Be prepared to take legal action on customers that won't pay.

Step 2. Ask for a Down Payment on a Big Order

When I was in the midst of restructuring my manufacturing business, the toughest money crunch came from a big order, something I wanted and dreaded at the same time. With limited cash, the purchase of inventory, and payment of wages, the weeks it would take to complete the work could have drained me. Then, the watch for payment began: at times a check arrived only hours before an unfunded payday. It's a tough way to live.

I once shared this dilemma with a good customer and asked if there was some incentive I could give him to secure a partial payment up front. We agreed on a discount and I billed 50% of the order in advance and, then when we shipped, I billed the balance. This deal released my other cash for ongoing expenses and really helped the company. I would not have suggested it to all of my customers; you must have a track record of satisfaction with any customer you approach. There is an issue of trust here.

One of my clients is a contractor who has suffered severe losses doing subcontracting work for very large jobs. On several occasions, the job came to an end and he wasn't paid in full. This caused serious cash flow problems and threatened his entire operation. While we worked on reorganizing his entire financial structure, he had a serious need for cash to fund his operation. We approached several of his large customers who had long-term working relationships with his company and asked for up-front payments to ease our problem. This was not usual procedure in the industry, but his customers considered our request a helpful accommodation and funded his recovery.

Step 3. Slow Down or Renegotiate Your Payables

Try to take extra time to pay your own bills, to hold on to cash as long as possible. Start by delaying payments 10 to 15 days: that may be a sufficient cushion, particularly if your receivables come in at an accelerated pace. Some vendors may not call, but don't use that as an excuse to avoid making any payments at all. You don't want to get noticed as a deadbeat, because once your vendors realize how delinquent you are, they may decide to take strong action and begin to require cash in advance, which will defeat the purpose of this tactic. If you can't pay a bill in full, offer to make a partial payment. Your creditors may not be happy, but you may be able to encourage them to accept reasonable offers.

> If you can't pay a bill in full, offer to make a partial payment. Your creditors may not be happy, but you may be able to encourage them to accept reasonable offers.

You may even try to work out a long-term payout on current bills and then pay new invoices promptly. This will help you hold on to cash and your vendor eventually gets paid in full and keeps a good customer through a temporary difficulty. You may be asked to pay interest on the unpaid balance.

Whatever strategy you decide on, you should always communicate with your creditors. Not taking or returning phone calls is a great mistake that can turn a late payment into a collection action or perhaps even a legal action. If you let your vendors know what's going on and when they can expect at least some payment, they are less likely to turn the account over to someone who will charge to collect it. Always communicate. If you have been sitting on your cash, you should be able to make at least a partial payment.

Everyone understands tough times. No one wants to lose all the money that a customer owes.

Never "Borrow" Money from the IRS

As you are slowing down payables, you may also be considering making your tax payments a bit late. After all, you've done it a few times accidentally and no one even noticed. My unequivocal advice to you is "Don't!" If you are short on payday, delay payroll for a few days for all or at least for some of your employees. They won't like it, but it is far less risky than making the net payroll and not depositing tax funds.

You may not hear from the IRS for weeks or even months about a missed withholding deposit, but when you do hear, you will be shocked by the penalties and interest that can be added. There are 5% initial penalties on failure to file and failure to remit and 5% per month interest on top of that. The tax due can double in no time. Bankruptcy lawyers have told me that over 40% of their clients are driven into court over tax problems. It is a slippery slope—don't take the first step over that line.

I have worked with a number of clients who fell into this dark hole and I have seen demand letters for hundreds of thousands of dollars. Owing the IRS money is not an easy problem to solve. While the government may accept a payment plan, it is just as likely to demand all the money due in 30 days—and it may go in and take it from your account by levy.

If you have already developed this problem, the worst thing you can do is ignore it or try to avoid facing it. If this is the first time it's happened to you, there is a real possibility of agreeing to a plan to settle your account. See an attorney immediately and have him or her start negotiating with the IRS before any enforcement action begins.

> *Tip* — Most government taxing bodies will allow you up to 24 months on a voluntary payback arrangement.

Step 4. Draw on Lines of Credit

A good banker is an excellent resource for a small business owner; you should cultivate this relationship carefully. Always be truthful with your banker, not only to enhance your credibility but because you never know how the banker may be able to help you during difficult times. Knowledgeable bankers know that businesses go through cycles and they won't be shocked if you tell them things are a bit tough.

Any written document you turn in to the bank must be accurate; it is never good policy to misrepresent the condition of your business. In some circumstances, to do so might constitute fraud.

If your company has been granted a line of credit, there is no reason not to draw on it during tough times. Even if your account is up for review and you think that your credit line may be reduced, it is yours now. It might even be a good idea to draw down the line and park the money somewhere. If your credit line is reduced, few banks will demand immediate payback and you will have the cash available for an emergency. If you pay a little back from time to time, you may not even get their attention.

Open a Second Bank Account

There is nothing illegal about parking money from bank A in a new account with bank B, and now may be the right time for that new business account. The money should not be in your personal account. Don't act as if you are trying to hide it.

It is not always easy to predict how your banker will react if your business doesn't begin to turn around and you need additional forbearance or even more capital. Some banks can be very accommodating, especially to long-term clients. But your particular branch manager may have just been burned by a loan gone sour and want yours off his or her desk to avoid getting noticed by top management for that reason again. Loan losses are an important form of evaluation for bankers; some would rather take no risks so that they show no losses. It may have little to do with you or your business. Try not to take it personally.

A second banker may have a different attitude and show a real interest in developing you as a new customer. This banker may be willing to be more liberal in loans and more competitive in rates. Banks become aggressive from time to time in developing new accounts and placing new loans. After all, interest from loans is a major source of bank income, so holding cash usually makes little sense. A new banking relationship may be just what your company needs.

Step 5. Identify and Sell Dead Inventory and Unneeded Equipment

The early stages of a business turnaround are not the time to liquidate usable but slow-moving inventory at below actual cost. If you know the merchandise will eventually sell at a profit, try to hang on to it. Selling out everything in a panic for cash is a form of liquidation that will only increase your losses and jeopardize your future. Control the impulse. You want to have a business left that is worth saving.

On the other hand, if you have products you will never sell or equipment you will never need, now is the time to turn them into cold, hard cash regardless of the discount. Money in your bank account is more valuable to you than obsolete inventory on your shelf or equipment that has to be stored and insured.

Call in an auctioneer or even a surplus buyer. There are some listed in every phone book and a large number of national dealers. If you have an extensive amount of inventory, try companies in the same industry in other parts of the country.

A very good resource is the many Web sites such as eBay that list general goods as well as specific types. More are coming online all of the time. These sites include page after page of listings from surplus liquidators. A review of these pages will give you the chance to see who might be likely to specialize in your type of inventory as well as what prices your excess inventory might bring. Always seek multiple offers and don't be shocked if you are offered 10% or 20% of the actual cost. Accept the best offer you can find, bank the money, and don't look back. The point is to stabilize your business enough to have the chance to move forward. Put the cash to good use to serve that purpose.

There is a balance sheet consideration as well in the liquidation of equipment and inventory at below market prices. If the inventory is still being carried at cost value and the machinery hasn't been fully depreciated, you will show a loss of income and an adjustment to assets. At a time when you need the cooperation and forbearance of your bank, this could cause them great concern. Work with your controller or accountant to determine the effect on your company before taking any action.

Step 6. Barter Instead of Buying

Every strategy in this chapter is meant to increase the amount of cash you will have to ease your way through current difficult times. You may also need to finance new opportunities for the future. This exercise is all about building cash reserves and holding on to that cash. Eventually

> *Tip* — Internet services such as eBay are good for selling inventory and equipment. You never know who might have real need for something you can't use. Cast a wide net on the Web.

you will look at ways to make long-term cuts in expenses, but in the meantime, consider whether there may be goods or services that you manufacture or provide that can be used to trade for goods and services that you need. This is known as *barter*.

You can join a formal barter group, but many of them require a registration fee up front. Joining one may not make sense if you'll be trading on a limited basis. What you can do is start your own program by approaching a vendor who is also a customer and see if you can trade goods or services on a more or less equal basis. Keep track of the exchange transactions and don't let them get out of balance. You don't want to be hit with a bill for cash out of the blue.

Several of my clients use this system very effectively. I have seen this most often with the media, particularly radio stations. They will trade on-air advertising time for those items they require, such as office supplies, printing, travel, and even restaurant use. It may be particularly helpful for businesses that deal in perishable items, such as advertising time or airline seats, that are lost if they are not sold. Use your imagination.

Remember, also, that simply because you are not paying directly for the goods or services of your vendor, don't use more of them than you can justify for your current business needs. Your long-term goal is to control costs, whether in cash or in trade.

How Your Business Affects Your Personal Life

What happens to your business happens to you. The two can seldom be separated because you have benefited from your financial success and inevitably you will suffer from any downturns. You know this because you have most like-

> *There may be sales tax implications in barter transactions and you may be required to record the revenue as income for any corporate tax. You should check with your state Department of Revenue or with your accountant.*

ly personally guaranteed the company's loans and may feel as if the entire debt could come crashing down on you at any time.

There are two things for you to consider even this early in the process:

- Conserve your own cash; you may need it.
- Don't commingle personal assets, even as a short-term cash infusion into the business.

Get Control of Your Personal Cash Needs

At the same time you are trying to store extra cash to protect your company, you should be doing the same thing personally. During the years that your business was doing well, you may have drawn a substantial salary. Now you might have to make decisions between paying yourself and paying a bill. If you are personally cash short, that decision will be made even tougher.

Once you have completed your analysis of the company and developed a projection of how long it will take to turn it around and how deeply you will have to cut into the

Prepare for the Crunch

My insurance agent shared his personal experience when he faced a critical business situation and immediately dealt with it by cutting his own personal expenses. The insurance company that had been his main source of commissions announced that it was no longer going to write auto policies in our state and the loss of this revenue could have had a disastrous effect on his agency. Along with some strong, extra effort at marketing, which minimized the impact on his revenue, one of the first things my friend did was cut back drastically on his personal overhead, including all memberships and purchases that were not necessary. He prepared for the struggle before it began. You should do the same.

expenses, you will have a better handle on any personal adjustments that will be necessary. While your circumstance is still in flux, however, it's wise to keep yourself liquid and flexible. It is tough enough to worry about the financial condition of a business; if you are personally in jeopardy, the stress may be unbearable.

Be Cautious About Putting Personal Funds into the Business

One of my clients kept his business alive by refinancing his home and summer place and putting all the cash into the company to keep it liquid. That was a mistake in the beginning and a mistake in the end.

The extra cash masked most of the symptoms of the problem and allowed him to avoid for too long, the reality of the company's situation. By the time he ran out of personal funds, the problems had become too severe to correct. At some point in the months before the business closed, he was no longer able to take any salary and he was getting crushed by two large mortgages. Finally, when it was over, there was no way to pay any of it back. The company was liquidated by the secured lender and my client had to help with the sale but received none of the proceeds. A painful lesson.

Consider carefully all these issues before you put personal resources into your business. You may need them for yourself, and you may only buy a little time, not enough to complete the job at hand! Instead, invest human capital to redirect and re-energize the business.

> *Tip* — Don't be the lender of last resort—you have the most to lose.

Use Your Cash to Stabilize Your Business and Yourself

The goal of any turnaround is to refocus the company in the direction of new business and profit. The first task is to firm the footing. Conserving cash is a good way to begin.

Chapter Key Points

- Make a plan to increase your available cash and ease your stress.
- Speed up receivables collection by putting a tough program into force—and keeping up with it.
- Slow down your payables with partial payments or short-term forbearance from creditors.
- Negotiate down payments from customers before you begin a big job.
- Draw down lines of credit that are already in place for your business.
- Develop a second banking relationship and try to negotiate better loan deals.
- Sell excess inventory and equipment that you will not be able to use in your normal operation.
- Use barter instead of cash; you may even develop new customers out of this system.
- Cut back on your draw at least temporarily and scale back your personal needs to accommodate this action without increasing your stress.

CHAPTER 6

PULL BACK MAJOR PROJECTS FOR REVIEW

PROCEED WITH CAUTION

One of my first major consulting projects was with a small manufacturer whose principals had initially described to me the need to increase sales and marketing efforts. Once I got into the company and did some serious investigation, I realized how deep and pervasive their problems were within the organization.

Most of their contracts were on razor-thin margins and their manufacturing personnel were so undisciplined that little work was done on time and within budget.

Equipment wasn't well maintained and there was always pressure from the same employees who neglected maintenance to replace older machines rather than fix existing equipment. A small loss was quickly turning into a hemorrhage of red ink. Everyone labored under the assumption that all they needed was one new hot-shot sales rep. In the beginning, I had lobbied for a stronger marketing plan before bringing someone else on board, but I soon realized that a structural change was required. At times I had to control the impulse to stand in the middle of the building and yell, "STOP!" Finally, I got the full attention of the owner and convinced him to take control and put everything on hold until we could determine which direction to go.

A Quick Fix Is Not the Answer

A company develops over the years. While it is doing well, everyone wants a part of the credit. When it begins to get into difficulty, no one wants to take any of the responsibility. Everyone begins to hope that one quick fix will solve the problem and that "everyone" includes the owner. But the fact is that, like a car or even the human body, when the first symptom of trouble is ignored, the situation can grow worse until it involves almost all aspects of the operation.

Even if you really believe that your trouble is localized in one or two areas, you must realize that looking for a "quick fix" is not the answer. I will caution you about the following:

- You don't have room for one more serious mistake.
- You can't take on a new line of business just to generate revenue.
- You can't afford to sell at a loss for long.
- Hiring new employees without looking at your structure isn't the solution.
- Don't send out the wrong signals.

A Company in Distress Can't Afford Another Mistake

One of the strengths of small companies is in the energy and the willingness to create change in the organization. One of the weaknesses is the tendency to act before the issue has been completely considered.

Sometimes the best thing to do is nothing. It's hard for most of us to exercise that discipline. Boredom is the enemy of most entrepreneurs. We have always welcomed the next big challenge of developing a new product or entering a new market as a sign that we are still in the game. But the weaker your company is, the smaller the margin for error: now you must keep that thought foremost in your mind.

Purchasing equipment that won't bring immediate return or hiring a new employee who will initially cost more than he or she earns could prove disastrous. Now is the time to be as conservative as you possibly can. It won't be for an extended period, just long enough to stabilize your operation, analyze it completely, and set a new course, if necessary.

As soon as you stabilize your company, your effort will be redirected to finding out what area or areas of your enterprise has brought you to this precarious situation. Until you've done that, any action may simply make the problem worse.

Here are some quick examples. If you have been under-pricing your products, hiring a hot sales rep will just allow you to lose more money. Buying equipment in an effort to attract new business may cost more than the profits it will generate, which may further weaken your cash position. Finishing an expansion that you once believed necessary may now be the opposite of what you really require. Instead of increasing your position in your current field, you may need a way to reorganize into a smaller business. Even if you have already expended some time and cash on the project, throwing good money after bad isn't prudent. Perhaps you should carefully slow down the whole process while keeping your investment intact. The time you take now will pay future dividends.

Even if the effort to stop a change in process is enormous, my advice is still the same. The first thing you must do is get a firm grip on the operation and be very familiar and comfortable with it before you change it in any way.

> *Tip* New products cost money to develop and market. They are a long-term investment. Don't fund them with short-term cash.

Increasing margins can maintain profitability when revenues are shrinking. 20% of a half million brings the same bottom line as 10% of a million.

Don't Take on New Business Just to Keep Busy

I'm not recommending that your company stays entrenched in the status quo, because I know as well as you that the business environment is always changing. Even if you maintain your existing business base, you should always be looking toward the future. But, even if your revenue has dropped, now is not the time to chase after new and unfamiliar work to find an instant fix if embarking on new ventures hasn't been your strength. You may need to redefine your organization, but take time before turning everything upside down.

I worked with a small contractor who had built a successful business doing a large number of small jobs for individuals and other small businesses. He had good equipment that he was able to replace regularly. Other larger contractors took note of that and began offering him a chance to bid on some big jobs as a subcontractor. It looked like a chance to expand. Unfortunately, a number of the jobs were

Expanding into Bankruptcy

A jewelry store in my neighborhood announced a big expansion into the antique business, which motivated me to stop in and see what was going on. The owner told me that over the past year his regular business had deteriorated and profits were almost gone. I asked him why he had decided on antiques and he didn't have much of an answer, other than his ongoing interest in antique jewelry.

Over the next few months, I seldom noticed any increased level of business at his shop—until I saw signs for a "going out of business" sale in the window.

He had increased his costs by purchasing an entire new product line, which had, in the end, generated no additional return. Now his already serious cash flow problem became fatal and he was forced to close his store. It's a tough way to learn a lesson in patience.

A Small Deli

Another of my clients was a small deli restaurant that had earned a steady income until a new strip mall opened across the highway with a tenant that had a slightly fancier operation. Ben, who owned the deli, had always considered starting a catering business but hadn't pursued it beyond doing special takeout trays because his hours already were long and he was always looking for reliable employees.

Serious competition from the other mall shop caused a 30% drop in sales, so Ben panicked and started his new catering service in record time. He lined up his first job in less than two weeks. It was an absolute disaster a Saturday evening informal dinner party that almost closed his business for an entire day to prepare. Only one new person was brought on board to serve. Ben came in early with another cook to prepare the food. By lunchtime, they still didn't have everything in hand, and they were neglecting most of their regular customers because there was no space left to cook individual orders. In the late afternoon, in a panic, Ben closed his restaurant three hours early to finish preparing for his catering job. When the results were in, the restaurant had a $350 revenue shortfall, Ben had worked a 17-hour day and, if he didn't count his own time in the cost, the catering job had broken even. Not a bright beginning! An exhausted and dejected Ben called me for help.

The fact was that catering was one of the answers for Ben, but not the first one. He couldn't afford to take on new overhead for personnel and additional equipment before he stabilized his existing operation, and he needed to study how he could handle the extra work of catering without hurting his deli business.

underbid and not completed properly and my client wasn't paid a substantial amount of the revenue he anticipated.

My most difficult problem in working with him was convincing him to take a hard look at what type of work he did well, and could make a profit on, rather than take every new job that was offered, just to maintain his cash flow. All new bids had to be carefully considered, because any further losses could have completely devastated his company.

You Can't Afford to Sell at a Loss for Long

How often have you taken a hard look at your balance sheet? Do you compare your net worth from one year to another? If you have been losing money for a few years, you are aware that the equity you have built up over the years has been eroding.

Cash flow is important to a business, but not if it's ensured at a consistent loss. Most new businesses have an operating loss as a part of the start-up costs, even established businesses that are diversifying into new markets. This is a cost you may not be able to afford at this moment. Even if you can, however, you want the time to think it through before heading out on a new path. If you work your way through the stabilization and analysis portion of your turnaround, your chances of success will be better and your new direction will have a better long-term implications for the success of your business.

In addition, the cash you are beginning to conserve and the funds you will create by cutting costs, and possibly liquidating unnecessary goods, can be used to fund the new project adequately. A well-financed launch has a better potential for success and you won't have to work as long to get it to that stage.

Freeze Hiring Plans

Now is not the best time to hire, even to replace someone, although in that case there may be some exceptions. If you need to fill a key slot, you should hire someone. But if others can fill the gap, perhaps that would be best over the short term.

In most cases, taking the extra time to review the operations of a department will be worthwhile. Perhaps if you

Tip — Productivity is the result of skill enhanced by training. It takes time and costs money to bring someone new up to speed.

did the job yourself for a few days, you would gain some insights into how it could be more efficient or even if it could be eliminated. For example, if you have one individual doing all the purchasing for your company, is it possible to allocate budget authority to a number of others so they can make purchasing decisions for their own departments? They would have a better idea of how much money is spent and may even show you ways to save.

As for any new employees such as the surefire, hotshot sales rep described earlier in this chapter, they usually turn out to contribute far less than you have anticipated. There are no saviors; even major league sports teams have found it almost impossible to find a single star that will make an average group into a winner. It requires the hard work of all the members of the team. Once they are up to speed, perhaps someone new will be the impetus to take it over the top. You must work on your in-place team first.

Even large corporations make the mistake of believing that, regardless of their structural problems, there exists somewhere a magician who can make all the troubles go away. Many have fired a qualified CEO because he or she couldn't cure overnight what ailed them. And even more have started down the same path, searching for one savior who would create a new vision and a return to profitability. It didn't happen. These companies spend a bundle to search for a magic bullet, but they don't always learn from their experience. That bullet doesn't exist.

Don't Send out Distress Signals—Create a Positive Spin

Whatever project you stop or job slot you leave unfilled, do so with a positive explanation. There are a number of ways to give the appearance of stability rather than panic:

- Slow down any projects gradually.
- Stretch out completion dates to delay acquiring any new costs.
- Keep in touch with potential employees even if you can't make a commitment now.
- Be open with current staff as to when purchases may be made or hiring freezes released.

The trick is not to cease your activity suddenly and without any justification. Don't cancel an equipment order without first inquiring about putting the purchase on hold for a later shipment date. Explain that you are doing some additional research before you make changes in your operation.

If you have almost come to the point of hiring someone, let your candidate know what is happening. If the hold is indefinite, say so, but if you would still have an interest in this individual at a later time, let him or her know that, too. The candidate may still want to be considered when your circumstances change and you may save time by having a qualified individual available when the time is right. Your explanation can be as simple as the fact that you are in the middle of reorganizing the department and don't want to bring in someone new until after you have refined a new job description.

Also keep your employees informed as to why you have decided to stop hiring for the moment. Give them some tasks to do to review their current work arrangement with the understanding that progress will resume after the review is complete and new plans can be created. Always talk about the future, set new goals, and keep those around you informed.

There will be many new opportunities for you to set your company in motion again, but at present you should keep actions in control and take the time to review your options.

Keep your actions positive. You're not pulling back to fade away. Rather, your role is to explore, to find new ways to move forward.

Chapter Key Points

- Review all new projects and hold off decisions until the company is stabilized and more analyses have been done.

- Put equipment purchases or expansion plans on hold.

- Analyze current business lines and new opportunities before deciding where your future effort may best be directed.

- Abandon all hiring plans except for necessary replacements.

- Keep believing in the future of your business and plan as if there will be one.

CHAPTER
7

CUT EXPENSES ACROSS THE BOARD

TRIM HERE, THERE, AND EVERYWHERE ◄

In the post 9/11 travel environment, the airlines saw the necessity for swift and meaningful cuts in every aspect of their operations.

Planes were grounded as flights were cut with the intention of flying people on fewer but fuller planes. Pilots and cabin attendants were laid off.

Food service was dramatically reduced to save money and brought back sparingly as markets demanded it.

Vendors were asked to cut costs as well and many complied to save their customers, as well as their share of the business.

Technology, such as online booking and check-ins at the airport, replaced people with digital equipment.

For some airlines these steps minimized the losses and some even turned profits.

But without these efforts, the entire industry was facing disaster.

Reducing Costs

The first step back from the losses that have been threatening your company's future is to slow the flow of red ink. One of the main reasons you put aside new projects is to cut back on your current outlay of cash. Unless you have embarked on some sort of major expansion drive that dramatically increased your expenses, this will not be sufficient. What will be required is a temporary across-the-board cut of all but the most necessary expenses. Since this is a short-term event, you can wield a big knife. The process goes as follows:

1. Set a percentage goal for your cuts.
2. Don't spare any department.
3. Try to combine jobs to cut wages.
4. Ask your vendors for help.
5. Cut your personal expenses.

Determine the Amount of Savings Required

Take a look at your profit and loss statement for the past three or six months. Go back long enough to get an accurate picture of what losses you have been incurring over an average month, not just a bad one. If you include a monthly depreciation figure, back it out of the statement for this purpose. Your concern now is the cash shortage you are experiencing, not the fully depreciated loss. Eventually, you will need to increase revenues and to cut costs enough to return to profitability. For the moment, though, you are attempting to stabilize your cash flow so that you don't go any further into debt; and you will accomplish this by a major cutback in expenses.

Use a Cash Flow Projection

You will need to create a cash flow analysis to find out what your target savings must be. This is different from a profit and loss statement, because it uses your cash income rather than sales as a revenue amount. In other words, even if your sales were $50,000, if you collect only 80% of those sales, your revenue is $40,000. Use a format similar to the one shown in Figure 9-1 and begin with your next month.

```
   1. Cash available (how much will be in your account for the
      first of the month)
 + 2. Collections (all receipts)
 =    Total available cash (all money available)
 – 3. Fixed monthly expenses (rent, utilities, etc.)
 – 4. Variable expenses (wages, materials, etc.)
 =    Cash available for debt service (loans, old bills)
```

Figure 7-1. Projecting cash flow

If your bottom-line number is a negative or less than your outstanding loan payment, this helps to form the percentage of expenses you need to cut. You also need to add an amount that will leave you able to make payments on old debts so that eventually creditors will be paid off in full. Plan to pay over a year if you can.

For the purpose of the example, shown in Figure 9-2, 1 will use rounded numbers as a guideline for your format.

Make This Temporary Cut Swift and Strong

This is not the time for putting into place budgetary changes that will be in effect for the long haul. At this moment you are attempting to conserve cash to get the breathing room you need to work on analysis and structural change. You may not have the time to go back for a

Cash on hand		$7,500
+ Collections		25,000
Available Cash		$32,000
Fixed Expenses	9,000	
+ Variable Expenses	23,000	
Total Expenses	$32,000	
Available for Debt	500	
− Loan Payment	800	
− 1/12 of Old Debt	1,300	
Shortfall	($1,600)	

FIGURE 7-2. Figuring costs. In this example, shortfall = 5% of total expenses and the required cut across the board is 5%.

second round of cuts and it is important as well that you appear strong and decisive. After you know what the necessary amount of savings will be, add a bit for a cushion and take out your knife. Nobody will like the sacrifice, but if all employees have to tighten their belts at the same time, they can treat it as a mission, not a punishment.

Don't Spare Any Sacred Cows

If you have chosen a percentage figure with a small amount of play, you must make your cuts on every line item to achieve the number you need. I have never seen a budget that doesn't have at least a few percent of waste in it; yours most likely follows that generalization. Sit down with your employees, describe the target numbers you are trying to achieve, take out the knife, and begin to make the cuts. Solicit advice on this matter because you want to have full cooperation.

Start off with items under your own control (sales

> *Some of the line items that merit the closest consideration are the administrative costs:*
> - *Travel and entertainment*
> - *Inventory (stock reduction)*
> - *Office expense (phone, postage)*
> - *General supplies*

expenses, for example, such as travel and entertainment) and volunteer to cut out all but the most necessary expenses. Take the position that this is a prudent act at this time—certainly not a major sacrifice, because many of your staff may feel that the costs of these items aren't justifiable. These may be the least understood costs in business. You must continue to stay visible. Ask for other ideas for reducing expenses and keep a running total so you know how close you are coming and what additional belt tightening is still needed.

Review all aspects of the business operation with those who are most directly involved. Can you reduce inventory? Can you save energy (and its cost)? Can you cut out some of the phone service? Don't stop at just cash savings; ask about other efficiencies as well. If you save time, you will save money.

You may have to share more about the financial realities of your company with your employees than you have in the past and it probably won't be very comfortable. But you also may be surprised at some of the valuable suggestions that employees will make to save time or money or both. People don't mind being told about a problem if they can be part of the solution.

Combine Jobs to Cut Wages

Combining several jobs into one will allow you to make cuts on staff. On the other hand, with computerized assistance such as voice mail, e-mail, and word processing, there are some jobs that have become less than full time. Can some of your employees cross-train on other jobs and ultimately make it possible to reduce employment levels? The savings from that could be enough to make your business breathe easier. You won't know unless you ask. Now is the time to replace warm bodies with efficiency.

A company in distress puts a strain on everyone associated with it, so the suggestions that involve increased workloads and possible layoffs should come from others, if at all possible. When talk of the need for personnel reductions originates from you, employees will all begin to think that their own jobs are in jeopardy. It may undermine the team spirit you're trying to inspire and that you will need to turn the company around.

What About Pay Cuts?

The first stage of a turnaround shouldn't last longer than four to six months, because if you can't stabilize your operation by then, your problems may need more major strategies, such as legal reorganization. Any pay cuts that are agreed to in this first phase will only be temporary and may be enough to buy time to change direction. You know how your pay scales compare with industry and regional averages. If you are already below them, any further requests from you will probably result in employee defections, which you certainly can't afford at this time.

If your current pay is at or above average, then consider this short-term measure. Use your absolute percentage number and inform your employees in advance of why and for how long you will be reducing their wages. There will be some grumblers among the group, but try not to let it get to you. Perhaps you can pledge to try to make restitution when circumstances change, but don't make any absolute promises. No one will really believe your intention, so it won't make the impression you want—and if you are unable to follow through at a later date, everyone will remember that fact.

If your relationship with your employees has been good and you have been open about the company's cir-

SECOND WIND

> **Tip** If you're operating under a union contract, you can't arbitrarily go out and cut wages without bargaining for a new concession.

cumstances, you may find more cooperation than you expect. On the other hand, if you've had an adversarial relationship, perhaps the effort isn't worth it unless the situation gets completely desperate. A business can deteriorate even further with disgruntled employees.

Cut Your Own Pay as Well

You will need to cut your own pay by a figure high enough to make a difference, but don't make a major point of it. Again, you're trying to motivate everyone to pitch in to help, not prove how "this is hurting me worse than it's hurting you." It's all relative.

You can't compare apples and oranges. Don't bring it up and it won't be discussed.

Ask Your Vendors for Their Cooperation

When GM was in the midst of losing hundreds of millions of dollars, it began a major restructuring that included asking vendors for relief. You're not GM and can't get away with any real pressure, but there's no reason not to contact vendors and ask for any cost-saving ideas they may have. Ask specifically if they might suggest new products that work as well as ones you are currently buying and be more economical. You never know what suggestions they might make and how it could affect your bottom line. Ask about any quantity savings if you order more and order less often. Is there a certain level of sale that will carry a prepaid freight term?

Be candid about what you need to do and indicate that you would rather work with your current vendors to get the savings that you need than find a cheaper source of supply. One of my clients found out that if he placed more

> You may be able to defer unpaid compensation for a later time. Talk to your accountant about the tax implications of this.

> ## Be Fair
>
> One company president I know made a major point of telling everyone how he cut his pay by 30% while he was asking them for a 10% cut. Since his life style indicated an income many times that of his average manager, the point was lost and his strategy even backfired, causing everyone to grumble after the meeting was over. His folks immediately cut their workload by 10%, which defeated the purpose.

business with a single material supplier, he would be able to work on a consignment basis that really helped his cash flow. He had access to a larger inventory and paid only for what he used.

Your Landlord May Be Able to Help

Don't forget your landlord. Even though he has a contractual relationship with you, a temporary rollback of rent may not be out of the question. If you're in a desirable location, you may be greeted with silence, but if your space wouldn't be easily rented to another company, a temporary accommodation may be possible. You could offer to add extra rent to the final few months of the lease after your business has had a chance to turn around. It may also help to pay the rent in two payments a month instead of one. Also, perhaps you could perform some work in lieu of rent.

When it comes to cutting costs, you should be ruthless—this is present survival and future growth that is at stake. What you accomplish now will have its return over the next few years, so rather than look at this as a retrenchment, view it as a consolidation leading to the next push forward.

Cut Your Personal Expenses

Your livelihood is very dependent on the long-term survival of your business, so this same across-the-board strategy should be applied to your personal expenses. You will have to take at least a temporary cut in pay and perhaps benefits, especially those that are discretionary, such as travel and auto reimbursements. If you have been living a somewhat lavish life style, you may find it difficult, but let me assure you that it will be harder if you put it off until you are behind in your bills. The added stress of personal bill collectors on your back can be devastating.

There are things you can do now to ease your overhead while keeping options open. If you belong to a country or private club, ask to have your membership made inactive for a year (or a season). If you have been a season ticket holder to a sporting or cultural event, sell one year's tickets while maintaining your rights to the seats. Any excuse about a temporary increase in workload is believable, and the reduction in overhead cost may really come in handy. If a car lease is coming due, consider trading down or buying a small car to use until things turn around. Talk to your family and ask for their cooperation. Family vacations may have to be scaled back and spending on your house deferred. It may be a sacrifice for a while, but it won't be forever.

Chapter Key Points

- Establish and implement an emergency cost-cutting plan.
- Determine your cash shortfall by analyzing your cash flow and determining how much it will take to meet debts.
- Cut all costs, not just a few; no department should be exempted from at least a token cutback of expense.

- Look at personnel costs. Can you combine tasks and reduce hours?
- What about temporary pay cuts? Be careful about how you present this step to workers.
- Talk to your vendors. Ask them for suggestions and let them know your goals.
- Talk to your landlord. A good tenant is worth keeping with some short-term concessions.
- Include your personal expenses as well. You will be cutting your own pay and you don't want to get behind on personal debt.

CHAPTER 8

CREATE A SUPPORT TEAM

DON'T GO SOLO

David Wilson didn't set out to be the "lone ranger." But starting his own construction company was more than a full-time job. Early mornings, he organized jobs, afternoons he worked on selling new work and doing estimates, and evenings he went over the paperwork. He spent what little free time he had with his family.

In early 2001, when business had become difficult, he had little in the way of a support team. He had concerns and even new ideas and no one to discuss them with.

One afternoon, his outside superintendent came back early to find David sitting in the office looking dejected. They began to talk and David slowly took this trusted man into his confidence.

Over the next few weeks, the two of them met with the company accountant to try to pinpoint what was wrong—poor estimates or poor performance. They added a consultant to the mix and later an architect who had given them a lot of work.

Over a three-month period, this formed the basis of a turnaround team that made great progress.

You Need Help

When your business was doing well, you probably longed for more quiet moments to be alone. Now, if you are typical of business owners facing difficulty, you are spending too much time isolated with your own stress.

You may not realize it, but your exile is really self-imposed, and it's caused by several factors. First, the necessary financial cutbacks you have made may have caused you to socialize less when expense is involved; you may have temporarily given up golf, sporting events, or even going out to dinner. A second reason may be that you're not sure if you really want to be in the company of others. The world around you may seem as if it's still on the move while you are immobilized. It's an uncomfortable feeling, but totally natural under the circumstances. And, unfortunately, you may be a bit embarrassed by your situation. This feeling is unfounded, yet it is one I see frequently among my clients. People tend to be their own hardest critics.

One of the characteristics that drive us into business for ourselves is the desire to be independent, but there are times, and this is one of them, when you really need the advice of others. If you have a board (even if the stock ownership is primarily yours), convene it and discuss current circumstances. Ask members to help you develop strategies for a turnaround; that's part of their role.

Here are a number of others that you may want to include in your inner circle and to involve in your decision-making process. Perhaps you can form an advisory group.

- The company accountant
- A good business attorney
- A friendly banker
- Key employees
- Trusted friends and business advisors

- Consultants
- Former employees (now retired, perhaps)
- Your insurance agent

Meet with Your Accountant

Many small companies have inconsistent relationships with their accountants. In some cases, all the accounting firm does is prepare statements without much comment; and in others, it primarily handles tax returns. Few small businesses can afford the ongoing participation and advice of a CPA—and few owners would take much of that advice if offered. If your relationship is constructive, your accountant may be of great help now. It is possible that the only action you'll have to take to tap this resource is to bring him or her up to speed on current conditions. Invite your accountant to your place of business so that the issues you are discussing become more tangible. Talk about ways to shore up the existing business first. Is there a way to generate more cash flow or profits that you haven't considered?

Have Your Accountant Review Your Financial Structure

A small contracting firm I worked with only briefly had six

Sometimes It's Easy

I worked with a restaurant that had an extremely competent CPA available, although he was called only when profits declined seriously. At that point, one of his first questions was about the last menu price increase, which had been made over three years previously. After much discussion, a new menu was printed with an across-the-board 4% increase. In the first month, only two customers mentioned it, but almost $60,000 was added annually to the bottom line—a good beginning to a turnaround. Needless to say, they're not all that easy.

loans that it was paying monthly. One loan was for a line of credit for operating money and the rest were for equipment purchases. The owner never discussed this sort of financial structure with his accountant until he began to have trouble making the payments. The first suggestion the CPA made was to consolidate all the loans and extend the payback period from the one to three years currently in place to five years across the board, using an SBA-guaranteed bank loan. The company's payments were cut by 40% and the relief was immediate. I was out of a job, but my client was on the right track. That was enough for me.

You and your accountant should take a hard look at your financial statement, particularly from the view of a banker or other lender. Has your deteriorating condition become evident? Are your current ratios sufficient to keep your loans and lines of credit from being called? If you had a strong equity base over the past few years, it may be that some time in the future you will have to deal with a "hardhearted" banker.

If you have not had a working relationship with your accountant, now it may be too late to try and develop one to make an immediate contribution. You don't have the luxury of time to work out communication and understanding of how you work and think and what your goals have been. Some accountants are more analytical; others are more creative. You need strategy, not micromanagement. At some point you will need the services of a good accountant. If you don't have one, find one.

How Lawyers Can Be Helpful During Tough Times

Most business owners call their company's attorney when they are angry enough to sue someone or have received

> *There is a special certification that some accountants earn called a CMA—Certified Management Accountant. These individuals are desirable because of their emphasis on operational issues.*

SECOND WIND

some threatening communication about action being taken against them. You may not think of your lawyer as a good business resource, but that is exactly what he or she might be. As members of the business community, lawyers have resources that may be of real help to a business in difficulty. They often know individuals who can liquidate inventory or equipment without making it public knowledge. They also know where some quiet investors might be. This could be a lifesaver if you are able to sell an equity share in your business to raise cash. And, of course, your attorney can help you negotiate and structure such a deal.

What may be of greater help at this time is using your attorney as a buffer between you and any vendors or lenders that you have been unable to satisfy. This will protect you from any anger or threats and often actually has the effect of securing forbearance from your creditors. Most of us know that collection threats are primarily bark, because the legal procedure to take a judgment and seize money or property can be expensive and time-consuming. Using these threats on a lawyer are a waste of time and energy, so you might be surprised when involving your attorney results in an offer from the other party to find a mutual settlement in amount and terms. Worth a try, don't you think? Remember, however, that you must make full disclosure to your attorney to get the proper help.

If a collection lawsuit has been filed, your time to seek legal advice is limited. You may have a defense, such as a dispute over the merchandise or the actual amount that is owed. You must file your answer in court so that you don't lose your rights. At least if you defend a collection suit, you will have time to figure out how you are going to pay off the amount not in dispute. Don't put these threatening documents in your bottom drawer and try to ignore them. They won't go away.

Tip — Lawyers bill on an hourly basis. Dumping all of your problems on the lap of an attorney can run up serious legal fees, just adding to your debt.

If you don't already have a relationship with an attorney, it is difficult to find one quickly, bring the person up to speed, and utilize his or her services effectively. It may also be costly, at a time when finances are one of your major concerns. However, unlike your accountant, who will be required as things improve, your attorney may be needed if business conditions continue to deteriorate. You will be better off to find, hire, and get to know a good commercial lawyer now than waiting until after a collection lawsuit has been filed against you. If your business is threatened by the actions of others, the legal advice you get (and, it is hoped, follow) may be the difference between survival and extinction.

Bring All Professionals Together for a Meeting

Few of us even think about introducing our professional advisors to each other, much less sitting down with them together and talking strategy. If you've had the foresight to pick good ones, now is the time to have a group heart-to-heart. Discuss your current situation and produce some contingency plans for the future. If you can afford it, plan to get together on a regular basis (weekly? monthly?) until the current crisis has passed and you feel less vulnerable.

Add to this group any other advisors you may have worked with and feel would have something to add. Is there a marketing consultant who would have strategy to contribute or a turnaround expert or a retired former employee? Be creative—the more firepower you can muster, the better!

If you have never needed or utilized strong outside advisors, it is never too late to put together some professionals who can really be of value.

First, find someone you really respect and trust—a

lawyer, an accountant, a consultant, or a business associate. A good and frequently overlooked resource is your insurance agent; he or she works with professionals frequently and should have some astute opinions about other advisors.

Then, you want to sit down and talk as candidly as you can about what you believe is the cause of your business problems. If you have fallen behind in tax payments, find a good tax attorney—immediately. Don't become so fearful of taxing authorities that you avoid them. If your cost accounting system is haywire, start off with a talented accountant. Make sure that you bring professionals in to help who have real expertise in the areas you need.

After that, you want to meet with those who have been suggested, to see if you feel comfortable with them. You also may want to bring two together over lunch to see how you all interact. The only downside risk is the cost of a meal and you are bound to go away with at least some advice.

How Your Banker Can Help You

Many bankers are sincerely interested in the well-being of their customers and are willing to go out of their way to be of assistance. But, it would be naive to forget that they represent the interests of the bank, so if you confide to them that you will be unable to pay back a loan, they must take steps to protect their interests. One small business owner I know came from a banking background, so she felt very comfortable chatting about her problems with her former colleague who was now her banker. Comfortable, that is, until he put a hold on her account against the line of credit she had outstanding. He was just doing his job!

On the other hand, if you are going through the early stages of a turnaround and trying to make decisions about the best hope for the future of your company, call on your

> *The Small Business Development Center is a federally and locally sponsored program with centers on almost 1,000 university and college campuses throughout the United States. They have excellent consultants available. You can find the center closest to you through the SBDC Web site, www.sba.gov/sbdc.*

banker as a potential source for information. He or she may be able to connect you with other customers of the bank as vendors, customers, and even joint partners. The more his or her client base succeeds, the better it is for the banker. If your bank manager seems to understand this, schedule a meeting to explore ideas.

Your Key Employees Are a Good Resource

I worked with the CEO of a small distribution company for six weeks about what he felt was "the brink of bankruptcy." In the beginning, we met out of his office. When I was finally allowed to see the business, no one was told that I was a consultant, let alone what my mission was at the company. I spent too much time trying to convince this owner that he had resources within his organization that could help us create a plan to get over a real tough spot. He had lost a large contract and was left with over $60,000 of inventory he couldn't pay for and didn't know where to sell. His major vendor was holding shipments of products he needed until this matter was settled. The company was becoming paralyzed by this situation.

Finally, after much wrangling, we called a meeting with the office manager, sales manager, and warehouseman. The CEO was surprised to know how much information his employees already had discovered and absolutely stunned that each one had already been thinking about a solution. The office manager suggested returning some goods for credit; the sales manager thought if they discounted products, they would be able to sell them and recover costs; and the warehouseman said the truck drivers who made deliveries would be interested in some of this inventory at a good markup over actual cost. By the end of the first session, all these ideas were implemented; within 10 days, $35,000 of the burden was lifted and the rest worked out over time. That relieved the immediate pressure.

There were also long-range issues to deal with, but now there was a new team to work on problems and solutions. I met with the whole group six times before completing the assignment, and afterward, I saw the CEO every six to eight weeks for review. He was thrilled with the new approach, and his financials prove it worked.

Your employees know much more about your business than you realize and maybe more than you like, but there is no way to avoid that. They need to hear the truth from you, and you really need their feedback. I've spoken many times about the isolation of a business owner with a distressed company—withdrawing into your office behind a closed door is the worst thing you can do, professionally and personally. And it isn't a good idea to keep key managers in the dark, either; their uncertainty will affect their work and poor job performance only adds to the company's overall woes.

Your Friends Can Become Informal Advisors

Many of us have friends and associates who are also in their own ventures. You may occasionally get together with such friends and associates, if only to complain about government regulations, your bankers, or perhaps your customers. Here is one more source of advice and support that you may not have considered. I don't know of one entrepreneur who hasn't gone through at least some tough times; most are sympathetic and have learned tricks to handle the problems they face. Try to meet over breakfast very informally and see if you can recruit a few of these hardy souls to form an advisory board. Get together as often as you need to and be ready to offer advice as well as ask for it. You may end up forming joint ventures or even starting new businesses together.

Ask for Their Counsel, Not Their Money

When a closely held company is short on finances, the owner will often try anything to raise the needed money privately. That includes borrowing from family and friends. I won't make a judgment about family. However, I will make one about friends—don't do it!

In life, if you are blessed with a good friendship, it is a rare and valuable commodity. During the difficult times, it will be your friends who will hold fast without judgments. This will provide a needed source of support. Making them equity partners in your business puts all that at risk. Even if they offer, consider it very carefully. If your business does not turn around and you can't pay them back, you've lost something worth more than money. I've seen these deals go all the way to court and become very damaging to everyone. At a time when you can't defend yourself, you may find yourself being attacked by someone you care about. It is very demoralizing. If you are not absolutely sure of how you will return the loan, don't take it.

A short-term, small personal loan isn't a big problem, but business loans are for bankers and other formal lending institutions, not friends. They serve a different role—that of supporters. Don't risk it.

> *Tip* — Do not ask for professional advice from a friend. Free legal advice can turn out to be wrong and very costly.

Chapter Key Points

- Finding good advisors is a critical first step to any successful turnaround.
- You should work closely with your accountant for both analysis and advice.

SECOND WIND

- You'll need a good attorney who will advise you of your rights and protect your interests.
- Your accountant and your attorney should work as a team: introduce them to that concept.
- Your banker may be a good source of advice, if the company hasn't gotten into serious trouble.
- Utilize the talents of your employees; they will appreciate your confidence and have much to contribute.
- Other business associates can help; put together an informal group.
- Family and friends are needed for personal support as well as advice—but don't borrow money from them.

CHAPTER 9

OPEN LINES OF COMMUNICATION

HONESTY IS THE BEST POLICY

> David Wilson (the construction company owner) and his super decided that their first step would be to talk to the rest of the employees and share the challenge of working to improve the outcome of the company.
>
> They began regular project reviews and learned by analyzing each job where there was room for improvement. Profit margins saw immediate improvements.
>
> Everyone had a far more optimistic view of the company and that eventually translated into happier customers and more secure suppliers. Instead of wondering what was wrong, the conversation became about what they could all do right.
>
> David felt far less isolated by sharing the problems with others and his energy and ability to be a motivated leader increased as well.
>
> It's difficult to admit that everything isn't going well, but often worth it in enlisting aid from unexpected sources.

Getting Real

There comes the day when you come to terms with the seriousness of the problems your company is facing. In the early stages, you are aware that current orders are slow, even inquiries are off, and cash is short more often than usual. There is no absolute definitive diagnostic test, no X-ray to take, only mounting symptoms. There is almost never one single moment of enlightenment in the early stages. Since you know the rhythm of your company, you know when something is wrong. But the optimist inside of you (and there must be a substantial dose of that just to be in business) believes that prosperity is just around the corner. Given all this as a backdrop, when do you begin to openly acknowledge your situation and with whom?

In the last chapter, I suggested that you work with your accountant and attorney as soon as you are ready to develop a strategy for a turnaround. I also strongly recommend that you include key employees in this process. Bring other outsiders up to speed on an "as-needed" basis.

There are a number of individuals and organization representatives whom you will want to include in your ongoing communication plans. Consider all those who may be affected by what happens to your business and plan when to involve them. Some of those may be:

- General employees
- Suppliers and other creditors
- Your customers
- Family and friends

Tell Your Employees the Facts as You Know Them

What about the rest of your employees? Depending on how seriously your situation has deteriorated, most of them will soon learn that something is wrong, if they don't already know. For those who work in the office, the signs may be irate collection calls, certified letters, or even a sheriff serving notice of a lawsuit. For those who manage inventory, it may be products no longer available to your company because of credit holds or lost credit lines. Other indications crop up all over: deferred maintenance, COD deliveries, personnel cutbacks, or even talk in the neighborhood. Other local business owners will often get angry when their bills aren't being paid, so word may get around.

If you are already aware that your employees are discussing the condition of the company, it's time to open your conversation with them. If you only suspect that word has spread, check it out with your managers. The optimum situation would be for all the information to originate with you, because it will be accurate and positive.

What you say is important—half-truths or unrealistically rosy scenarios may come back to haunt you. Explain what led to the current situation (e.g., the loss of a big customer, the failure of one of your products to catch on, or general economic conditions), describe it as completely as you feel appropriate as well as what you are doing to turn it around, and give at least an estimate of your time line. Be honest: tough times don't end overnight, but they do end.

What Your Employees Tell Outsiders May Be a Critical Factor in Your Comeback

From my own perspective as a customer, the problems at many companies are evident from the attitude of their employees, regardless of what management is issuing for public consumption. Workers may be angry and customers aren't being treated very well. The more that trend continues, the greater the likelihood that the company's troubles

> *You want your employees to stick with you and even exert some extra effort during the rough periods. A well-informed employee is a motivated one, and uncertainty is likely to cause the flight of the talented people you really need to manage a successful turnaround.*

SECOND WIND

Creating Team Spirit

One of my clients operated a health club during a very long and extremely difficult reorganization that several times looked as if it wasn't going to succeed. The owner is a charming and open woman; she may not always have felt like sharing all the ups and downs, but she believed her employees had a right to know, so that's what she did. At regular intervals, everyone got together for an open exchange, all questions were allowed, and answers were offered.

A team spirit formed among this group that was at least 50% responsible for the ultimately successful outcome. That isn't to say that the hard work and sacrifice were easy, because they weren't. But working as a group with a single goal makes it challenging and worthwhile.

---

will mount, and they may very likely end in a bankruptcy filing.

That's not what you want for your business. You need a strong customer base now more than ever, and the care and consideration your clients receive from your employees are critical to that retention. Workers who are getting less and don't know why or even those who have partial knowledge that the company is in trouble but no information from the source are not likely to give that service. These employees become so wrapped up in their own concerns that the best interest of the company is not served. Don't let this happen. You can do much to prevent it by opening up your own lines of communication with your employees.

> *In the post-9/11 era, airlines were hit hard. Employees were worried, which impacted on the way some companies treated employees. This made flying even more difficult and a recovery longer to achieve.*

Talk to Creditors

It may not be easy, but you have to talk to creditors. Unanswered collection calls are the quickest way to see your company fall into a legal morass that will end badly. Not all creditors are polite and cooperative. Some may actually be abusive. But whether it is the creditor or a collection agency, providing no information inevitably takes the action one step further into a legal process, until you may end up in court or even in bankruptcy. It only takes a few creditors with claims totaling a mere $10,000 to put your business into involuntary bankruptcy.

But why let it go that far? If you can't pay your bills in full, work out a plan of partial payments or extend the deadline for sending a check. The only way to do this is by talking to the human collecting the bill. A series of "He's in a meeting" or "Can she call you back?" will only bring suspicion, not buy time. You have to do that in person.

I was recently in a meeting with a client and their controller began going over outstanding receivables. Every time we began to discuss a company that wouldn't take any calls or return any, the conversation became very serious about what enforcement options might have to be exercised. In contrast, if the controller had some contact with a principal of the business, it was likely that we agreed to give additional time for an amicable solution. The fact that you continue to communicate and eventually pay off a debt may serve you well in the future if you want to get credit again.

If you are really uncomfortable about having a conversation with your creditors, perhaps you could start the dialogue with a note or short letter. One caution here is to avoid making any promises.

Other Benefits of Communication

There are other benefits you may not have realized from communicating with creditors. You may reach some individuals who have real commercial savvy and may be able to suggest general business ideas. If they are vendors who primarily sell within one industry, you might even find some marketing assistance. You may be able to sell your own

Involuntary Bankruptcy

Chapter 7 and Chapter 11 of the bankruptcy code allow creditors holding claims against a business or an individual to file for relief, under certain circumstances, by filing a petition. This is known as *involuntary bankruptcy*.

If the debtor has fewer than 12 creditors, then any creditor with an unsecured debt (no collateral) of at least $10,000 that is not subject to a bona fide dispute may file the petition. If the debtor has 12 or more creditors, at least three creditors whose claims total $10,000 above the value of any collateral must join together to file the petition.

Before the court will accept the involuntary petition and issue an order for relief, the creditors must prove that the debtor either is not paying debts as they become due or has entered into some sort of non-bankruptcy liquidation.

---

slow-moving inventory to someone else in your industry and at least recoup your cost. A vendor may be able to suggest whom to call. You won't know what help is available if you don't take the incoming calls and discuss your situation.

More Good Reasons to Talk to Creditors

You will want to have an impact on what is said about your company by other businesses in the area or in your industry, but you can't accomplish this from a position of silence. You need a chance to explain the circumstances of your company's current situation and then describe your strategy for changing that situation. Your own spin on the subject will be much more positive than one put forth by someone unfamiliar with your circumstances. People will talk—why not participate in the conversation?

Your company may not make the recovery you expect or it may take longer than you anticipated and creditors will be forced to wait an unreasonably long time before getting paid. If all they've heard is silence, they are likely to take strong action, including legal action. Once lawyers get involved, it adds costs and risk. Several creditors can join together (or be brought together by one attorney) to put your company into involuntary bankruptcy. A creditor is less likely to take this type of major action against someone with a recognizable name and personality. Don't give them any reason to think of you only as a message or a person always "in a meeting."

Communicate with Customers

Your customers will also almost always find out about your difficulties, sooner or later. Their information may come gleefully from your competitors or from an awareness that your inventory is lighter than normal or that you may be experiencing constant equipment failures. Sooner or later, your business situation will become common knowledge.

Should you stonewall any inquiries? My recommendation here also is against that tactic. I would suggest that, instead of silence, you opt for optimistic honesty. Be candid about how difficult the current business environment has become, but be sure to inject your plans for the change and revitalization of your company. Your customers will come away feeling that they have heard the truth from someone in the know and feeling assured that the situation is only temporary and that they still have a vendor to rely on.

You may even be able to use your troubles to your own advantage—starting with the famous "fire sale" to raise cash. Be careful that a planned inventory liquidation sale doesn't take on the look of "going out of business." If your customers begin to develop new buying habits, it won't be easy to win them back.

Sample Letter to Supplier

September 29, 2003

Dear Mr. Supplier:

You may have noticed that recently our payments have been slower than you normally expect from our company. Our cash flow has been strained by a colder than normal winter and lower than expected sales. We are all working diligently to correct our problems and hope to be back to a better schedule soon. We will be in touch shortly to give you an update on our progress.

We appreciate our long-term business relationship and thank you in advance for your cooperation.

Sincerely,

Owner, XYZ Company

SECOND WIND

> *September 29, 2003*
>
> *Dear Customer:*
>
> *From time to time, business conditions become more difficult than most of us would like. There are always a number of reasons and a number of solutions as well.*
>
> *We are currently going through a major restructuring to make our company more efficient and better able to serve your needs quickly and at competitive prices. During this transition, there may be temporary disruptions in our service or levels of supplies. If you notice any difficulty working with us, please bring it to my attention personally.*
>
> *We have always appreciated your business and look forward to many years of mutual benefit.*
>
> *Sincerely,*
>
> *Owner, XYZ Company*

Don't Be Afraid to Ask Your Customers for Help

I can remember a particularly tough time for my small manufacturing company, when I wasn't sure if I could finance the next order. A particularly big piece of business, though desirable in terms of revenue, meant working capital requirements that strained every available dollar. Finally, in desperation, I admitted the problem to the customer I had known personally for a long time. I volunteered that an advance payment would make a major difference and I would be willing to offer a discount over the 1% or 2% traditionally given. The customer accepted my offer; not only did it ease my cash burden, but the incentive was sufficient to encourage this customer to offer us other large contracts on the same terms. I subsequently made the same arrangement with another customer, with equal success.

Talk with Family and Friends

Those who are close to you will begin to notice a change in your behavior once the grinding stress of your situation begins to take hold. To leave them in the dark about the causes of your distress is a disservice both to them and to yourself. This is another case where lack of information can cause others to come to mistaken conclusions. Also, whether or not you realize it, the advice and support of friends and family are particularly important at this time.

One of the first signs you may experience is sleep disturbance. I went through it and most of my clients do also. Even now, I still wake up between 4 and 4:30 in the morning, but now I use the time to write and plan my day. I've even met with clients as early as 6:00 a.m. If you've started this pattern, don't fight it—learn to live with it. Make available other time to catch up on your sleep and plan work to do if you're up through the night. My own turnaround took over three years, and I learned to leave reading material or other work on my table before I tried to go to sleep, so that if I woke up it would be right there and I could almost pretend that I had set the alarm so that I could finish my project.

The rest of your family will begin to notice your night stalking and other stress-related behaviors and they may worry. That's a burden you don't need now. Do what you can to describe what a "business nightmare" means in personal terms and assure them (and be assured yourself) that nothing lasts forever. This will end.

It's also important that your family members cooperate financially. Everyone must curb their spending now and they have a right to know why. It's a good life lesson, since most of us have at least one setback in our working lives, whether for ourselves or someone else. A child who isn't told the truth may see your denial of something he wants as punishment, which isn't the case. A child who is asked to assist may feel good about his contribution to the family's well-being. The same is true of a spouse, who should be included, not protected.

Friends Are a Source of Counsel and Support

Your friends will also notice the change in your life style. You may have canceled vacation plans or dropped a country club membership or other things along those lines. The people you normally traveled or socialized with may suspect the reasons but not know how to approach the subject. It's often a good idea to open the dialogue with those you are particularly close to. Don't wall yourself off because you are feeling a sense of failure at not being able to keep up. You can find new activities that require less expense but may prove to be more fun. And you won't become isolated, which is very important at this time.

Friends who are in business themselves may be a good source of advice on how to analyze your situation, how to expand your market, or perhaps how to find a more cooperative banker. It's almost always better to incorporate the opinions of more than one person in your decision-making process. However, there are at least two exceptions to this rule.

The first would be when you are protecting more information than you are sharing. You may be acting properly and cautiously to withhold some data from others, but keep that in mind when they come up with ideas. If they don't have all the pertinent facts, the advice is flawed, although parts may be of use. For example, describing how the bank is making life difficult for you without also confessing that you are months behind in payments isn't fair or constructive.

The second is free but incomplete legal advice. Friends who are also attorneys may think they are doing you a favor by giving you suggestions without charging a fee. If it's out of their specialty, it probably isn't very effective, and if it's only surface advice, the dangers can outweigh the benefits.

Keep Your Spirits Up and Your Outlook Positive

Anyone who has gone through a serious business reversal knows how gut-wrenching it can be. Allowing yourself to lose contact with vendors, customers, employees, and even family and friends is a serious mistake. Keep your lines of contact open. Keep a "can do" message out and you will begin to realize the possibilities.

Free ... but Costly

I had one client whose best friend was a partner in a major law firm. He advised his friend to take a tough and sometimes devious stand against a bank that was causing pressure on the business. When the bank officer finally became infuriated and pressed legal action, my client's friend couldn't back up his advice with a defense because his firm represented the bank and it would have been a conflict of interest. The company ended up in liquidation. The friends are speaking but no longer socializing.

Chapter Key Points

- There are business lines of communication to keep open with voluntary and honest information.
- Talk with employees, to maintain their cooperation by answering their questions and asking for assistance.
- Talk with vendors, to prevent unnecessary legal action and encourage them to assist you in keeping credit available.
- Talk with customers, to keep up their confidence in your company.
- Talk with family members, to inform them of what is happening and to secure their cooperation and support.
- Talk with friends, for their advice, support, and continued association.

SECTION III

▲ ▲ ▲

CREATE A STRATEGIC PLAN FOR SUCCESS

CHAPTER 10

PREPARE A COMPREHENSIVE FINANCIAL ANALYSIS

A COMPLETE FISCAL CHECKUP

The difficulties you are experiencing in your business may have been precipitated by a single problem or there may be multiple areas of trouble. Left untreated, even a single chronic problem will affect the other aspects of your operation until the entire company becomes involved. The best way to create a turnaround is to determine and treat the root cause first and then attend to all the ancillary symptoms. You start by conducting a complete analysis, one that begins with looking at historical financial performance charts that compare year-to-year results. These will give you an indication of where the trouble started and a clue as to how it can be corrected.

The most typical assumption is that most business problems can be solved most easily by more sales and that will cure all that ails the company. While this is often part of the problem, it is an oversimplification of what constitutes a business success. The gross sale number is a key indicator, but it is the profit generated that is used to retire debt, invest in new assets, pay investors, or form a cushion that is of critical importance to survival as well as success. If you are losing money in your operation, higher sales may only afford you the opportunity to lose even more cash and hasten the end of your business.

SECOND WIND

In the beginning of this book, we were dealing with the issue of cash with the emphasis on staying liquid enough to meet obligations. Generating extra cash is a short-term solution, and if a turnaround does not occur that will refill your coffers with profits, you won't survive for the long haul. And that is the point of this effort.

The Main Issues of a Financial Analysis

In preparing your financial analysis, you must include the following information:

1. Compare year-to-year results.
2. See if your expenses are in line with current sales.
3. Calculate your breakeven revenue.
4. Identify which expenses you will have to reduce and by how much to turn a profit with little or no growth.

If your accounting is in a computerized database already, doing this work should not be much of a problem. Many software spreadsheet packages have analysis features built in, and you just have to enter year-end data. Even if you are on a one-write or manual bookkeeping system, it is not that difficult to do a comparison chart. It is important to make sure the categories are consistent from year to year; it would affect your analysis if expenses were allocated to one account in 2001 and completely changed to another account by 2003. If they have been refined, readjust them to similar categories for the purpose of analysis.

Tip — Both QuickBooks and Peachtree will give you an income statement by percentages. That allows easy year-to-year comparison.

Compare at Least Three Years

Your first step is to spread out three years of numbers in a side-by-side format (see Figure 10-1). This allows you to compare the actual cash amounts over a period of time rather than poring over the results of a single year. If one number looks either very large or very small, you should research the details of that account. This system allows you to take a hard look at your expenditures on a year-to-year basis to get some idea of where they may be out of time.

The example in Figure 10-1 shows a company with 2001 sales revenue of $1.8 million. It is easy to see that the sales have fallen by 20% over the three years that are covered by

	2001	2002	2003
Sales	1,800,000	1,600,000	1,450,000
Cost of Goods	1,260,000	1,136,000	1,044,000
Gross Profit	540,000	464,000	406,000
Expenses (Administrative)			
Wages	305,000	288,000	262,000
Benefits	18,000	20,500	22,500
Rent	23,000	23,000	23,000
Utilities	6,500	6,600	7,100
Sales Expense	45,000	54,000	38,000
Telephone	23,000	19,500	18,500
Insurance	6,000	6,200	5,800
Depreciation	7,500	6,800	5,900
Interest Expense	20,000	18,000	12,000
Office Expense	30,000	40,000	35,000
Warehouse Expense	15,000	21,000	18,500
Total Expenses	499,000	503,600	448,300
Net Profit (loss) before taxes	41,000	(39,600)	(42,300)

Debt Repayment (beginning of year)			
250,000 @ 8% for 5 years			
200,000 @ 8% for 4 years			
150,000 @ 8% for 3 years			

Debt	200,000	150,000	150,000

2002 sold assets to pay debt
2002 did not pay principal

FIGURE 10-1. Financial analysis income statement

this report. The owner of any business who has experienced this drop in revenue is already aware of it, and his first instinct might be to stop here and not analyze further. He may walk around believing that if only he could increase his sales, all his problems would be over.

The line-to-line chart in this example does send up several areas to investigate. A year-to-year comparison shows growing costs of benefits that should be looked at more closely. Wages are down (note that the amount is less than the 20% of revenue loss) but also important is that the cost of benefits is up. These two numbers should increase or decrease at the same time. There may be other glaring inconsistencies on your own statement. Take a hard look at the details.

Convert Numbers to Percentages

Step 2 is to transform these numbers into their percentage form (Figure 10-2). Each number is converted to a percentage of the total amount of expense. With your numbers in this format, you can compare both your profit margins and expenses on a year-to-year basis.

Studying a report such as this may help you find the answers to what ails your company. Are your profit margins remaining steady or are they dropping? Are the problems in the gross profit margins or are your administrative costs too high for your current level of sales?

If at least one of the three years that you are using as a comparison wasn't a year of healthy profits, go back and find the last year that did make a net profit. Restate the figures from that period to conform with the ones on your chart and use it as a model. Figure 10-2 of my example is a very telling document.

	2001	2002	2003
Sales	100%	100%	100%
Cost of Goods	70%	71%	72%
Gross Profit	30%	29%	28%
Expenses (Administrative)			
Wages	56.48%	61.42%	64.53%
Benefits	3.33%	4.42%	5.54%
Rent	4.26%	4.96%	5.67%
Utilities	1.20%	1.47%	1.75%
Sales Expense	8.23%	11.64%	9.36%
Telephone	4.26%	4.20%	4.06%
Insurance	1.11%	1.34%	1.43%
Depreciation	1.39%	1.47%	1.45%
Interest Expense	3.70%	3.45%	2.96%
Office Expense	5.56%	8.62%	8.62%
Warehouse Expense	2.78%	4.53%	4.56%
Total Expenses	92.30%	107.62%	109.93%
Net Profit (loss) before taxes	7.70%	(7.62%)	(9.93%)

FIGURE 10-2. Financial analysis using percentages

The very first thing I notice is that the cost of goods (which should be a stable percentage) has gone up and the profit percentage has gone down. The gross profit is 2% less in 2003 than in 2001. This factor alone would have wiped out most of 2001 net (before taxes). The major point to consider here is that if this company's sales grow back to earlier levels it will still be in jeopardy.

This chart shows that there are a number of other very important areas to investigate and improve. Wages have become far too high as a percentage of costs. In 1991 total wages and benefits were almost 60% of expenses; now they total 70%. Have salaries gone up while revenue has gone down? Are there too many managers on the payroll?

Also, in this example is evidence that the office and warehouse costs as a percentage of expense have gotten out of line. In 2001, they totaled 8.25% of expense, but by 2003, they total almost 13.25%, an increase of about 60%! You may not have seen this in the raw numbers, but it becomes very obvious in the percent conversion chart.

Make a Line-by-Line Analysis

Step 3 of this process is to make a line-by-line analysis (Figure 10-3). Review areas where you are performing well, not just areas where there are problems. Note that I have made a comment on every line of my example, and you should do the same. It will force you to pay attention to all the aspects of your operation even if you did not normally do so on a regular basis. Ask others in your company to explain their own areas of responsibility. Any questions raised must be investigated further.

I have made comments along the lines described in my review for the early analysis statements, but in Figure 10-3,

---

Sales
    Cost of Goods – direct costs have increased
    Gross profit – down by 2%

Expenses
    Wages – up by over 10%
    Benefits – too high to maintain
    Rent – need more sales in space
    Utilities – not out of line
    Sales expense – why has spending gone down?
    Telephone – OK
    Insurance – OK (but seek competitive bids)
    Depreciation – set amount, not cash loss
    Interest expense – refinance at lower rate?
    Office expense – too high, needs cutting
    Warehouse expense – excessive for sales

Net Profit (loss) – trend is dangerous

FIGURE 10-3. Line-by-line financial analysis

I have added a few more. The sales expense described here has been going down in numbers even though it is up as a percentage. I would want to consider whether this company's marketing efforts are sufficient to generate the new sales they need.

Also, I have noted under the insurance category that the company should go out and seek competitive bids. In this case, I was hoping to create some steps to be taken to bring this operation back into line. All the managers should have a copy of this chart.

See if You Are at or Above Breakeven

One other serious issue to consider is what your current breakeven (no loss/no profit) revenue number is. This is the level of revenue you must have at your current profit margin to pay all your current expenses.

To find your approximate breakeven number on a monthly basis, you divide your total expenses from the past year by 12. While accepted accounting principles would have you consider the payment of interest and taxes as "below the line" items not to be considered as general expense, for the purpose of a turnaround, you should add them.

Next you need to establish your average profit margin percentage on sales (gross profit minus net sales). For example, if your gross profit on $1,000,000 of sales is $300,000, then your percentage margin is 30%. If your total expense is $750,000, you will need $2,500,000 to break even (expense divided by gross profit percentage). See the breakeven worksheet in Figure 10-4.

If the breakeven number you have calculated is possible to reach, you may try to grow your way out of your present circumstance. If the sales number seems remote, then consider how to lower it by raising profits and lower-

> **EXAMPLE 1. BREAKEVEN WORKSHEET**
> Overhead Expense
>   Rent
>   Utilities
>   Wages
>   Office Expense
>   Insurance
>   Taxes
>   Interest
>   (Other expenses except depreciation) $750,000
> Gross Profit Margin   30%
> 30% of $2,500,000 = $750,000
>
> **EXAMPLE 2. 2002 STATEMENT**
> Expenses = $492,000 (less depreciation)
> Gross margin 29% – 29% of $1,700,000 = $493,000

FIGURE 10-4. Breakeven worksheet examples

ing expense. However, it is important to focus on one thing at a time. Don't take the shotgun approach of trying to change everything all at the same time.

Has Your Overall Sales Volume Decreased?

Whether your industry is downsizing or experiencing a period of flat growth, changing times as well as changing buying patterns will put pressure on your overall gross revenue. With less money coming in, there is inevitably less to be allocated to pay bills, and that creates pain. Your sales will not come back on their own—opportunities for new sales will increase during a general economic recovery, but your company will still have to pursue new sources of customers.

Take a realistic look at where your markets have been in the past and who your customers are as well as how their buying habits may have changed to determine where new sales may be found. Then analyze your current position. Is the overall market you serve growing or fairly static? Can

---

The Four Most Likely Problem Areas to Review

1. Overall sales volume
2. Gross profit margin (pricing)
3. Overhead expense
4. Debt service (interest expense and principal payment)

you increase your revenue by adding new product fines? Is the only way you can increase your volume to severely cut prices? Can you exist on low margin sales? What marketing costs will be involved in producing new sales?

As I've said earlier, assuming that higher sales are the single answer that will result in an instant turnaround is a mistake. If you are at breakeven and your gross profits are stable, additional revenue at current or even lower margins will surely help. But if your profit margins are too low, increased volume may result in higher losses and bring you closer to your demise. Consider this as only one piece of the puzzle.

If the company profiled in Figure 10-2 sells more at current operating costs, its losses will only increase. The airlines constantly fill seats at less than cost, believing that their overall revenue gain will ultimately help. What has been happening in reality is that full-price customers have been using lower-cost tickets and the red ink continues to flow. If you are giving your product away (not making any profit), stop now and overhaul your entire operation.

When cyclical industries such as cars and steel do not return to previous highs, a recovery may mean a lower level of activity than pre-recession.

Are Your Gross Profit Margins Sufficient?

If your gross profit margins seem very low or are on a steady decline on a year-to-year comparison, that may be the real culprit in your case. You should measure your company against industry averages (these numbers are available through trade associations and in published works, the major one by Robert Morris Associates) and determine how close your actual profit margins are to similar-size companies in your field or industry.

If you have been very aggressive in the market to spur on early fast growth, you may now find your business grossly underpricing its goods or services. However, if you have been a supplier to others long enough to establish a satisfied and somewhat loyal customer base, now may be the time to phase in a price increase.

A small manufacturer I worked with in my own business always took work at low margins because he wanted to achieve rapid growth. Not only was he often the low bidder, but his service was exceptional because he (and his crew) were willing to work long hours and over weekends to meet customers' demands. After keeping the same price list for three years, he reluctantly raised everything by at least 5% and worried about what would happen to his volume. At that point, due in great part to his fine reputation, it continued to increase.

Pricing of a product or service is part science and part art. You should not be afraid of charging a fair price, but you should be aware of where your competition is and how it will affect your overall revenue. Some price increases result in lower volume. However, lower volume at higher margins can in fact be more desirable.

> *Tip* — 30% gross of $1 million is $300,000, and 20% gross of $1.2 million is $240,000. Which profit figure would you prefer?

Is Your Overhead in Line with Revenues?

It is easy to become accustomed to the monthly bills you incur and not think too much about whether or not they are in line with your revenue or how you would be able to reduce them. At some point, your revenue must cover all your fixed expenses (rent, utilities, administrative wages, interest, etc.) and that may not have represented a problem to you in previous years. However, if your sales fall or your profit margins drop, just meeting these obligations can become an ongoing nightmare. This is one of the issues you must analyze. If your overhead percentage is growing and taking with it all your profits, this is an area for further analysis and corrective action, which will be covered in detail in Chapter 15.

Is Your Current Debt Service Too High?

Perhaps you are still paying off your start-up loans, and your growth hasn't been as fast as you had predicted at the outset. Few businesses meet their own rosy projections. You may have incurred debt for an expansion that didn't show the accompanying increase in sales that you had projected. Most difficult of all, you may have been borrowing operating capital and now be at the end of your credit line and unable to pay it back out of current cash flow. Be tough on yourself when you consider your debt situation. Too high a debt load is serious but not impossible to solve. What it will require will be tough negotiations and perhaps legal advice.

You need to determine, as well, whether your goal is to reduce debt to meet your current operating levels or to plan to grow enough so that revenues will increase to meet debt. I have worked with companies that have made each one of these choices, and they both are possible. What is required from you is a realistic assessment of your company and its potential. Is the demand for your product or service growing? Are you competitive enough to get a bigger share of your market? Ask tough questions; the answers are important.

Determine What Needs to Be Changed to Become Profitable Again

If you have effectively analyzed your comparative statements, you should have a handle on where the problems are centered and where you should put your priorities. The next step is how to focus on the specific areas of problems and how to begin to develop a plan of action for change.

Chapter Key Points

- Take the time to review company operations before planning your next step.
- Spread three years of statements side by side.
- Do a percentage analysis.
- Compare line by line.
- Determine if gross profits are high enough.
- Analyze overhead.
- Review all current debt.
- Determine your breakeven revenue.

CHAPTER 11

THE ELEMENTS OF A PLAN

YOUR ROADMAP TO SUCCESS

One of the most important tasks of any entrepreneur is to take the time to make a plan and to put it in writing. And it is one of the jobs business owners try to avoid. But even if you didn't write a full plan when you started your company, now is the time to realize that this is a critical step.

Before you go roaring off to take action, you must plan out the changes you wish to make. If you attempt them all at one time, you will create chaos all around you and that will serve no one's interests, least of all the business you are working hard to revitalize. You must take results from the various phases of your analysis and determine a step-by-step strategy to deal with the most pressing problems.

> *A business plan does not have to be a perfect specimen of literary genius. Committing your strategy for the future to words will help you think about it in detail and that is what you are looking for.*

Create a Plan

The elements of a good plan include the following:

1. Identify your main goal. What will the company look like when you are through?
2. Clarify the top priorities necessary to meet that goal.
3. Establish a reasonable time frame.
4. List steps in the order in which you plan to take them.
5. Establish how often progress will be reviewed and by what standard it will be measured. Set reasonable benchmarks.

1. Identify the Goals for Your Company

After reviewing the recent operating results of your company, you should have a good idea of what new goals you would be comfortable with over both the short and the long terms. These will often differ from one company to another. In some cases, goals may involve a commitment to growth so that you can sustain your overhead and current debt service. In others, goals may be just the opposite—a plan to cut expenses and pay down debt so that the company can operate profitably at current revenue levels. Your strategies are based on general economic conditions as well as current industry climate.

Bob Johns operated an offset printing company that had recently made an enormous equipment purchase. There was no choice: staying in business meant keeping up with the latest and largest press you could handle. The loan payment was brutal and the whole company almost crumbled under the weight. The only strategy that would work here was to plan for growth—higher revenues generated the cash flow needed to service debt. Of course, profit margins had to be kept intact as well.

On the other hand, Mickey had a construction company whose main customers were larger prime contractors that did major building projects. The whole field had slowed: a good bit of big work, a new stadium, and airport upgrades had been completed and little was planned for the next 18 months. Mickey's game plan was to become smaller, lower overhead, and take on less extensive work that still could be profitable. He had serious negotiations with his bank and landlord to get to this point.

Your goals must be clear—first to you and then to the others who will be involved in making them happen. If everyone understands where you are trying to go, you can all get on board and try to row in the same direction. Loosely based concepts leave too much margin for misunderstanding.

2. Establish Three Top Priorities to Meet Each Goal

There are several ways to achieve any goal, but since you are the one in charge of this company, it's your job to set the priorities to see the results you expect. Down the road you may want to begin other projects for improvements, but for now, you have to be very specific about what you want to change in your organization and how.

For example, if your goal is to pursue a smaller but more profitable business model, then your three top priorities might be the following:

1. Cut overhead costs across the board, including personnel. Reduce costs of unnecessary perks.
2. Close borderline operations.
3. Target a different market. Change customer base.

Or, for another example, if your goal is to grow bigger

and increase your overall cash flow, your three top priorities could be the following:

1. Increase marketing efforts to increase sales.
2. Lower prices along with reducing the cost of products or services.
3. Restructure debt to lower monthly costs. Gross margins may be lower.

While some of the steps overlap in these two efforts, these two companies are going in two separate directions. That is why you have to define your goal and you must choose the top three priorities to pursue.

I have worked with both methods and find they each have good possibilities and involve risks. Shrinking a company may make it less vibrant and eventually there could be little left to operate. Growing a business is also a risk, because the increased sales may not be there as quickly as you would like and the profit margins may be smaller. But they are both within reason to pursue and you will definitely increase your chances of success by advance planning.

> *Remember to think in percentages, not gross numbers. Lowering the percentage of costs compared with revenue raises the percentage of profit.*

3. Decide How Long It Will Take to Complete Your Program

You must determine how many phases it will take for you to complete your turnaround program and how much time you will allocate to each step. I assume you realize by now that you didn't get to where you are currently overnight and you won't get back to where you want to be in a matter of weeks or even months. The first phase of this program, described in the previous section, is meant to give you time to accomplish the real efforts of your turnaround.

You can plan on at least a year to see definite results in your operations, but some progress should be evident in the first three months and certainly a greater portion in six months. You must give the timing some consideration and decide on the time frame for each phase of your program.

This is the main reason that turnaround consulting projects tend to involve long-term engagements for those who do them. Even when we assume that a project has a short life span, it usually ends up taking months longer than anticipated. Many of the changes seem to be mechanical, but they all have a human component. People do not act quickly and they certainly do not change overnight. Be patient; prepare for enough leeway to allow for success even if it is slower than you would like.

4. List Each Step Involved in Carrying Out Your Plan

Each one of your priorities has a multiple-step requirement to complete. Your plan should list the major aspects of these steps and perhaps the interim time frames for each.

Perhaps your goal is to restructure debt to reduce costs. With interest rates lower now than they were several years ago, that may make sense for most companies. The task here is not as easy as going into your bank and asking for a consolidation loan as a consumer might do. You may find yourself completing the following steps:

1. Review all outstanding loan documents to determine any payoff fees and any loan requirements that identify the assets pledged as collateral.
2. List each loan and each payment required. Also include the current interest rate.
3. Have a current appraisal done on all assets that will be used to secure any new loan.
4. Do a restated profit-and-loss projection using any

new loan as the debt service; you must show that your operations can sustain the new loan payments. This step and the first three are important elements of any loan package. You must complete them before you go on to the next task, which is the most important.

5. Meet with a number of bankers as well as other lenders such as the SBA or other government agencies that have loan programs, to see if you qualify.
6. Complete paperwork, wait for approval, and close the new loan.

This six-step assignment could take up to six months or more and, with little exception, no step can be completed before the one that precedes. You must come to terms with this and use your plan to think this through in advance.

5. How to Schedule a Progress Review

Early into your turnaround, you will be meeting with advisors and managers very frequently. It is one of the natural responses to the feeling of impending crisis. After the ini-

Periodic Review	
Who is responsible?	**Time to complete**
Task 1. Controller with attorney	2 weeks
Task 2. Controller	1 week
Task 3. Owner to hire appraiser	3 weeks
Task 4. Controller, owner, accountant	4 weeks
Loan package should be ready to go in 30 days. Schedule meeting.	
Task 5. Owner, accountant	4 weeks
Task 6. Owner, attorney, accountant	4 weeks
Goal is to close new loan in three months.	

tial pressure is released, the number and frequency of these meetings will decrease. Your job is to keep the momentum on track so that you and others will complete all the tasks.

Once you have set priorities and established the steps required by your strategy, you must set up specific times to come together with those involved to review progress, deal with any setbacks, and make sure you're still on track toward the goal.

Each one of the priorities should have a similar progress review strategy and the overall goal should also have an interim review process and standards of measurement.

If your intention is to grow revenues by 10% over the next year, then you should measure your success quarterly. Be realistic about your expectations and when and how it is likely to happen. If you are a retail operation, for example, a good bit of your volume comes over the holidays, so don't expect to start in September and see success in December. Begin the plan in May and review progress each quarter. By Christmas, your plans should be bearing results.

Chapter Key Points

- A good plan is a critical element of any turnaround.
- After you have taken the time to analyze where the problems are, create a step-by-step strategy to correct them.
- Identify the new goals.
- Create a list of priorities.
- Set time lines for completion.
- List steps in detail.
- Schedule regular progress reviews.

CHAPTER 12

A NEW MARKETING STRATEGY

KNOW HOW TO GROW ◀

When Acme Printing decided to buy a new and bigger press, they knew that substantial growth was a necessity to pay for the purchase. A strategy was in place before the equipment was delivered.

The increased (and faster) capacity meant they could do more work for existing customers because they could handle bigger runs. There was very little they couldn't accomplish, so any customer that had outgrown their previous capacity or would not let them quote because of their size would now be a potential buyer.

The time had come to announce this "new and improved" level of manufacturing and they did it with style. Letters, postcards, and attractive examples of their work were circulated to those they knew or who knew them. Acme was particularly interested in those who put out a catalog or companies that did direct mail marketing.

A sales force followed up with personal visits and the level of quote requests rose dramatically.

If you already have determined that your costs are in line or your fixed overhead is almost impossible to reduce, the imperative for your company will be to grow its way out of the current crisis. Make sure that your profit margins are adequate, because cash flow can mask serious profit problems and further weaken the company. Just desiring (and needing) increased sales revenue isn't going to get you there. You will need a well-thought-out and well-implemented marketing plan to be successful.

Your company should have a written marketing plan. If you don't have one, that is the place to start. You can read entire books on the subject or take comprehensive classes, but what follows are some of the basics you should know. Enlist the assistance of your staff members who have knowledge or expertise. As in the business, the writing matters far less than the concepts.

The Basic Elements of Your Marketing Plan

There are a number of areas you need to review before revising your current strategy or creating a new one. Some of the questions you want to ask follow:

1. Who are your best customers? Do they have demographic similarities such as age, income level, or location? Or if you are a business-to-business company, is your product or service more suited to customers of a certain size?
2. What are the features and benefits of your company that make a customer choose you over the competition?
3. Are there other customers who fall into the same category who are potential clients (both demographi-

cally and as a match for features and benefits)?
4. What is the best way to make them aware of your business?
5. How can you develop a cost-effective strategy to accomplish the task?

1. Who Are Your Best Customers?

Many businesses open their doors to manufacture or sell a product or service without knowing exactly who their target customers will be. If that scenario has been a part of your company's history, you know how difficult it can be to try and market yourself to virtually everyone without having a specific customer type in mind. And in some cases, even if you did know exactly who your customers were when you started your company, with time the customer base may have changed dramatically. Change is a constant in the modern business landscape.

The manufacturing company I operated for 21 years produced and sold safety products to industrial end users. When I took over a business, it had a large number of clients so I didn't think that I would have to devote much time to considering where our customer base really was. Within 10 years after I took over the operation, almost 50% of our original customers had closed completely or experienced serious cutbacks. By the time I realized that I had to find a lot of new customers, it was almost too late. I consulted with a small retailer who had been selling the same type of merchandise for years while the neighborhood where he was located changed dramatically. All the demographics, including race and age, were now different. He was friendly and well liked, but no one wanted the type of goods he carried. A complete revamping was required to bring his business back to life.

When is the last time you reviewed where your sales were originating and determined what information you could derive from your current sales data? Unlike a start-up, you now have a business history to use as a basis for some in-depth analysis of your customer base. What common traits can you identify among those who have chosen to do business with your company? Use the demographic checklist to draw your customer profile.

By drawing a profile of those who have made the buying decision in favor of your company, you will produce a road map to finding the most likely new clients. The narrower the target, the likelier you are to hit it.

2. What Benefits Make Customers Choose Your Company?

If you're the chief salesperson for your business, then you should understand what is special and unique about your company. Interestingly enough, these may not be the main drawing features that cause others to patronize you. For example, you may believe that your restaurant has the best food in town, but your customers may come because you are close to where they live or work. Once you have your customer profile, then you should be able to analyze why they have chosen you. Is it a special product line? Service or training that you give along with your product? Fast delivery? Convenient location? Are you the lowest price in town?

There are two or three main reasons that you have attracted your customers and you want to identify them so that you can expand your marketing efforts and begin to grow again. Even if the answers aren't readily apparent to you, they are there in the company records or even the knowledge of your staff.

A Demographic Checklist for Business-to-Business Sales

If you sell to other businesses:

- What is your customer size—large companies or small businesses?
- Where are they located—regionally or nationally?
- What type of business are they in?
- What is their management structure?
- Do they have a purchasing department?

A Demographic Checklist for Retail Sales

If you sell to individuals:

- What are the ages of your customers?
- What are their marital status and family size?
- What is their family income level?
- What is their education level?
- What is their ethnicity?
- What is your geographical drawing area?

> **Tip** You can register to become a project of a university business class or go out on your own and hire business students to work on your survey. These are answers you need because they form the base of your strategy.

You can find even more information in the form of a market survey; staff can do this or you can hire an outside marketing firm to conduct your survey, although this can be expensive. Four students from a business school spent a semester on this type of project for me and their insights were excellent. The value of students is that most people will readily speak to them and tend to give candid answers. I even found out why some people didn't do business with my company.

3. Are There Additional Customers to Develop?

The next phase of your analysis is to determine whether you can continue to grow by developing additional customers similar to the ones you have or whether you will have to change or expand your business significantly. For example, if you already have a major portion of your existing market (e.g., 40% of all the pizzas in your area are bought from your shop), then you are going to have to be innovative to increase your sales. It could be something as basic as enlarging your product line or the services you offer or you may have to expand your location or open a new one.

If, on the other hand, you have only a tiny portion of the available business, this fact may be personally frustrating to you but the good side is that there is a lot of room to grow. Aggressive sales and marketing campaigns should work for you. Expanding your revenue will in many cases turn your business back to profit. Before you begin, you must be convinced that an expansion is possible without massive infusions of capital. If it will take an expensive advertising or promotion budget and you don't have the money to do it independently, you may have to look at partnerships, alliances, or even a sale to someone who can fund the required growth.

4. What Is the Best Way to Attract New Customers?

Does your company have a program in place for regular communications with your existing customers? If not, I can almost guarantee that your company does not have a plan to develop new customers. If you have reviewed the potential opportunities for expansion and determined that growth is critical for your survival and future, a plan should be a high priority with you at this time.

> *See how the fast-food chains have expanded their food offerings to attract those who didn't want only a hamburger or a piece of fried chicken.*

There is much written material about various types of marketing, from "guerrilla" or low cost to top of the line. Since your company is unlikely to be in a position at this time to throw money at a problem, you will want to choose both your method and its implementation with great care. Regardless of the direction you choose, the first step is to decide to whom (what type of potential customer) you are talking and what message (the important features of your company) they should be hearing. You are developing a targeted market to go after. Again, this is work that can be done by others, but if cost is the issue, you and your staff can do it.

There are a wide variety of methods to help potential customers become more aware of your company. The following list should give you some ideas of the alternatives you could consider.

Advertising Methods for General Public
1. Direct mail
2. Brochures
3. Yellow Pages
4. Newspaper

5. Radio and TV
6. Signs on your building and vehicles
7. Joining organizations
8. Speaking opportunities
9. Supporting a team or an event

One-to-One Promotional Strategies
1. Personal letters
2. Special discounts
3. Telemarketing
4. Canvassers
5. Direct sales calls
6. Web site
7. Tip clubs

These should trigger some ideas for you. You should pursue the ones that seem to be most appropriate for both your message and the customer you are trying to reach.

5. Is There a Cost-Effective Way to Market Your Company?

Finally, you should decide what cost per sale or cost per new customer would be acceptable, so that you can set a budget for your marketing efforts. Determine the profitability of each new customer or additional sale and determine what amount of that profit potential should be committed to new customer development.

If you have earned profits of $50,000 on the cumulative sales to 500 active accounts, your average profit per customer is $100. It would be imprudent to spend $10,000 to develop 50 new accounts at this time because it would take years to earn back your investment of $200 for each new account. Your goal now is a faster return on your dollar expenditure. In the future, long-range development projects are always worth considering. For now, keep the expense to less than 20% of your expected return. You need to retain new profit, not spend it.

Don't be deterred by a low budget. With desktop publishing capabilities, e-commerce, and cable television channels, all sorts of marketing concepts are possible at a fraction of what they once would have cost. Instead of giving up or giving in to spending money you don't have, take the time to read one of the many books available on low-cost marketing or take a course at your community college. Once you get into the middle of a spirited campaign, you will probably find it to be more fun than you assumed. You're in business because you believe in what you do. Here's your chance to tell others about that belief.

Project a Positive Image

While you are analyzing your current market position and deciding if your major efforts should go in the same direction, keep in mind that to neglect any marketing is a serious mistake. If your decision is to focus on the internal workings of your company, don't concentrate on that issue to the complete neglect of the image and message you are transmitting to existing clients as well as potential new customers.

When a company gets into some difficulty, that fact often becomes common knowledge. If you do not develop a plan for at least some external communication, customers

Chapter Key Points
- Take an analytical view of how your company is marketing to new and existing customers.
- Identify your best customers.

> - Make sure that you are promoting the most important feature of your business.
> - Find any new market opportunities for your company as it is operating now.
> - Design a cost-effective marketing program.
> - Customer communication is an important component of a successful business.

will begin to wonder what your long-term intentions are. You can prevent this problem with a program of regular communication and promotion of new products and new ideas.

CHAPTER 13

A CHANGE IN OVERHEAD EXPENSES

GET IN SHAPE FOR THE LONG RUN

> **W**hen I took over a family manufacturing company in the early 1970s, we were busy as we made safety clothing and new laws had just come into place that created a demand for our products. A few short years later and my business life had been turned upside down.
>
> The mid-1970s recession was serious and deep and began structural changes in the industrial customers we had served for 50 years. They closed operations—some temporarily and some permanently.
>
> I had to restructure my entire operation. I cut overhead by shrinking my office staff by one and using a mechanic "on call" rather than employing one full time. The production supervisor became a shipper as well. We had been renting an extra space for storage and we let the short-term lease run out. I was also able to term out a line of credit under a special SBA program for women. The tough times didn't last but my company did—I operated it for over 21 years, until I sold it in 1993.

If you have analyzed your statements and believe that your gross profits are in line but your expenses (fixed or indirect) are too high, that's where you should focus your attention next. In the first stage of your turnaround, you may have responded to the need to cut all expenses for a short period of time. But now for the long haul, what you should do is change the focus and identify the costs that are out of line and determine how to reduce them and keep them down permanently.

Review Each Line Item in Your Overhead Expenses

Take a close look at the detail included in every line item expense, even if you think you already know what they are. Review them even if you believe that they can't be altered. You may have assumed that expenses such as rent are just a fact of life, but that isn't always the case. You should take a look at what you are paying per square foot and then review how much of your space is really needed. You may have moved into space with an idea to expand and now, instead, you need to contract. This is the time to face this reality. A turnaround plan includes strategies to lower costs in every category, including rent.

As you review your overhead, you should consider other line items, in addition to rent, that you may have viewed as unchangeable. It may be possible to reduce the cost of your telephone service or other utility. Administrative wages may have appeared to be an absolute necessity before you began this process, but there are savings in this area as well. Even if you can't, at the moment, think of any ways to create savings, if you see a cost that you believe to be excessive, make a note of it and give some attention to a plan to money-saving ideas in that area.

One of my clients had very high employment costs (e.g., unemployment tax, worker's compensation, and insurance). These costs were based on industry standards and his company's history. He was aware that these costs were preventing his business from being competitive on quotes and the lost business was seriously affecting his bottom line. After much investigation, we found an employment leasing company whose business was to hire my client's employees, pay their wages and benefits, and lease them back for a fee. The leasing company enjoyed a substantial benefit in costs (on unemployment tax as well as a good insurance package) and the whole process saved 10%—enough to make the difference. This type of service is available in most major cities.

> *Tip* — How about outsourcing payroll and other financial record keeping? This will allow you to reduce staff.

Determine the Value of Your Sales Expenses

Sales and marketing expenses may seem to be very flexible costs, and it can be difficult to determine the exact value of many of these activities. This category will include items such as:

- Advertising
- Promotions
- Travel
- Entertainment
- Printing and mailing marketing material

At a time when cash is short, it may be all too easy to make extra deep cuts in these areas, but doing so could end up as a serious mistake. And by the time you realize it, changing the strategy won't be instantly possible.

Retaining current clients is critical: they need to see and hear from you. In addition, the only way to develop

> *Try hiring part-time workers or, if possible, independent contractors. They receive fewer benefits and work on an "as needed" basis.*

prospective customers is to get the opportunity to let them know about your company and its product or service. Getting the message out costs money. Not getting the message out may cost sales.

Any analysis of your current costs in these areas must be done with an understanding of what your competition does along the lines of advertising or entertainment. Remember that you must stay prominent in your customers' eyes. But now you must spend wisely.

As I look back on my 21 years in industrial manufacturing, I now realize that I did far too little entertaining. That is because early on it wasn't easy for a woman to take one man or a group of men out for dinner or a sporting event. Over the years, it became easier, but I never developed the habit. When business was soft, my competitors that had a greater presence with customers retained more of the available business. Entertaining is important and I recommend investing in it wisely.

You can measure your sales expense in terms of cost per customer or cost per transaction. The choice you make should depend on the type of business you operate and the market you serve. If you sell to a limited number of customers, use cost per customer. Otherwise, use cost per transaction. The formula would be the following:

$$\frac{\text{average monthly sales expense}}{\text{average number of sales}}$$

For example, if your average expense is $2,500 and you have 500 sales, then your cost per transaction is $5. Compare that with the average value of each sale. If your monthly gross volume is $75,000, divide that by 500 and you will find that your average sale is $150. Your $5 transaction cost translates into a sales cost of 3%. If your profit margin is 25%, this may be reasonable; if your margins are 10% or less (such as a travel agency), this may be high and you will have to address it. Conversely, if the number is very low, perhaps you aren't doing enough to promote your company. You know what your customers demand and what expenditure may be necessary to develop new accounts, so this is a call for your own instincts. Balance good marketing with cash conservation.

Review Your Administrative Costs

You must also measure your administrative costs against a fixed productivity factor, just as you measure your sales expense. How much overhead cost are you maintaining to transact your day-to-day business? You might translate it to a cost per order, which should include processing the order, billing it, recording all aspects of the transaction, and ultimately collecting the account and making payments to cover the costs of your operation. Your own salary (or at least a portion of it) and other managers' wages are also part of this cost. Divide your total overhead by the number of transactions to find out a cost per order. Then you must decide whether the expense to handle the administrative side of your business is in line or too high. Streamlining your operating procedures or outsourcing some of this work is a way to cut the cost. There are others that we will also discuss.

Involve Your Managers in Overhead Review

If your company has a talented controller or office or general manager, he or she can be the point person in a cost-benefit analysis. You first want to determine which items should be put up for scrutiny and then delegate the research. Once you begin considering what course of action must be taken, you should include in the decision process the individuals whose departments will be involved. The leadership is yours, but you should solicit and consider contributions from others.

Remember that the managers involved in reviewing overhead costs may be impacted by the decisions you make, so they may be inclined to pull punches and not give you their most candid opinions. Managers do not like to have their budgets reduced or, worse yet, their jobs eliminated. If you are aware of an overhead area that may require very serious and deep cuts, you should be up front with the managers whose job security may be in jeopardy. Perhaps they can move to a different assignment or you may still be able to ask them to help if you allow those who will be impacted to seek other employment opportunities while the changes are ongoing. It will be easier for them to find a new job while they are still employed. Your sensitivity and respect for others during tough times will be long remembered. On the other hand, your secrecy or lack of loyalty will also be remembered by those who stay.

Don't Create Unnecessarily High Stress

It is never easy to face difficulty and find solutions. The early stages of awareness are confusing and everyone is concerned about the outcome. Your employees also feel the stress deeply: it can become serious and cause conflict among people who should be working together to achieve a single positive outcome.

If you engage in finger pointing, that is, accusing others in your organization of spending too much money, you won't be creating an atmosphere conducive to finding solutions. Your job is to determine where the problems are and correct them. It's in everyone's self-interest to work for the future, not recriminate about the past. Your job is to motivate and lead by example.

Some Costs Are Subject to Legal Constraints

Your business will have fixed monthly expenses that are covered by legal agreements and binding contracts such as rental agreements, equipment leases, supply contracts, and labor agreements. And the costs covered by one or more of these may be just the expense that is burdening your company.

In addition, in some instances, not only are the contracts legally binding, but they may have cancellation penalties or payment acceleration clauses that make them very expensive to rescind. This is the time to seek the advice of an attorney. First, you will want to understand the actual costs of these clauses. (Few of us, unfortunately, review them in advance.) Second, you will want to know if there is a way to avoid this type of penalty. Contracts often contain escape clauses for various types of nonperformance and to activate them may require documentation on your part over a period of time. Check it out now so you will be ready when the time comes to take action.

Increase Productivity and You Will Increase Profit

While you are considering how to cut costs, you should also be looking at ways to increase productivity. If output goes up, cost per item or transaction goes down. Don't neglect this consideration as you make your review. Also, review current technology to see how you can invest in productivity.

> *Most reasonable creditors will allow a company in financial distress to make a financial settlement. They usually realize that if you are pushed into a bankruptcy they will be forced to accept one.*

> *Modern, easy-to-use software can add dramatically to the efficiency of your accounting, administration, sales, and shipping departments.*

Tip Many carriers such as Federal Express and UPS will offer free hardware and software for large users.

Can your salespeople increase the number of calls they make by using contact management software? Can they help out with administrative or shipping duties by entering instructions with orders? Can general office staff increase their tasks to include work normally done by part-time staff or outside service? If you manufacture, can your factory use idle time to produce products as subcontract work for others? Is there work for others that you can take in to increase your output per employee?

These are a few of the questions you should be asking yourself. When looking at overhead, don't just use a slash-and-burn approach to reducing costs. Use a surgical knife, not a machete. If you combine this approach with an increase in sales and/or margins, you can achieve some dramatic results.

Review All Your Debt

From start-up loans to equipment or auto loans to short-term lines of credit, it is not unusual for a company to have several loans that it is paying off at the same time. You may be paying interest only on a demand note or a fixed principal-and-interest payment on term loans, but you should review them all.

Although the basic rule is that a company should not borrow money unless it has the profits to pay back the principal, many start-up and expansion loans are granted with the expectation of future earnings. At times, your bank may have been willing to extend a short-term line of credit to smooth over the rough spots. Many companies find themselves unable to retire these notes and they convert them into term loans with a regularly scheduled payment. If the profits don't return, these loans can become a real burden to your cash flow. The debt may jeopardize the entire business. Something has to be done.

The Contractor and the Equipment Loan

The most difficult case I've seen was a contractor who started with an equipment loan of $150,000, went on to a $300,000 line of credit for working capital, and ended up with over $500,000 of debt. Payments squeezed his cash flow enough that he wasn't able to pay many of his subcontractors and they made claims on his bonds. We began to work on the debt load very late and weren't able to restructure any of his loans so that the company could generate the needed cash flow to continue operations. I believe that even six months earlier, there were options to pursue, but they eroded with time. He was forced to sell out to a major construction firm to avoid bankruptcy. The lending company paid suppliers and then took action covered by personal guarantees.

Questions to Consider in Reviewing Your Debt

There are a number of important questions to ask and answer in order to analyze current debt conditions.

1. What is the current debt total?
2. What is the current term of each loan? How many payments remain?
3. What interest rate are you paying? Is it fixed or floating?
4. Is the debt secured? Is the current collateral value equal to the outstanding balance?

What Is the Total Amount of Your Debt?

Your review of total debt is important to determine the solvency of your company. If you have a mortgage that belongs to the company or lease purchases for equipment that can't be canceled, include them in your total debt. An analysis is valuable only if it is complete.

When Does the Loan Mature? How Many Payments Remain?

You will also want to consider the term (length of time) that your loan was originally written to cover. The shorter the term, the higher the monthly payment. Stretching out a loan for a longer time may curb your ability to borrow additional funds for the near term, but you could substantially increase your cash flow by increasing the term and making lower monthly payments. You could use the extra cash for increased marketing efforts that would have long-term benefits.

What Interest Rate Are You Paying?

Do you know the interest rate on each loan, including any lease-purchase deal you may have? If your company is still paying on older loan instruments that were not pegged to prime, these may have rates far higher than are currently available. Virtually all leases are at a high rate because they aren't issued by the primary source of the funds. Lease companies borrow money themselves and must add a few percentage points as their own profit margin. Consider the effects of a lower interest rate on your monthly payment.

Are The Loans Secured?

As you review your loans, you should also determine whether they are secured or not. If the lender has a lien on a specific piece of equipment, then determine whether the value of the equipment currently is less than, more than, or equal to the current balance of the loan. A loan that was written to cover all general assets may have been considered secured at the time, but may not be now if the value of those assets is less than the current balance of the loan.

For example, if a loan for $200,000 was written at a time you had $150,000 of receivables and $100,000 of inventory, it was secured at that time. If, after a period of poor business conditions, your receivables are now only $80,000 and your inventory only $50,000, then any loan portion over $130,000 is actually unsecured. This is important to know, because any court-supervised reorganization will likely force your lender to accept less for the portion of its loan that is no longer secured and the bank understands this reality. You may need this information as a negotiating tool.

Know Where You're Going Before You Begin

By this point, you have done a thorough examination of the current operation of your business. Now it may seem to be the time to roll up your sleeves and dive in to make all sorts of decisions and changes. But wait! Don't do anything before you have a complete plan ready to implement.

It's impossible not to be impressed by the military success of Desert Storm; it should be a guiding lesson about strategic planning. The troops were in country for months before the offensive began and the win was stunning. Even if you think you know exactly what needs to be done (you may have really known for some time but just didn't do anything about it), don't start before your whole plan is developed.

Decide what your goals are and determine your priorities—that is, what has to happen before your company is once again nurtured back to health. Your analysis should have highlighted the major areas for concern. The chapters ahead will give you ideas on how to correct each of the problems you need to address.

Chapter Key Points

- Review each line item of your current overhead costs to see where you can save.
- Review all fixed costs, even those such as rent that you believe can't be changed.
- Determine the cost of marketing and sales per customer.
- Analyze your administrative cost per sale.
- Include managers in both the analysis and the implementation of any plan.
- Keep the stress level in check; everyone in the organization may be feeling under siege.
- Consider all your debt—the total amount as well as the interest rates and the terms.

CHAPTER 14

A LOOK AT PRICING STRATEGIES

WHAT FIGURES MAKE ENE?

> One of my clients was a restaurant that was attempting to reorganize. A beautiful place that had begun as a "fine dining" establishment, prices were moderate to high and service and quality had to meet those expectations. But business had been off and debts, including unpaid taxes, had mounted. In an attempt to increase volume, the owners decided to lower menu prices and create a more family-type environment, which they felt might be more popular in the area. Their problems started immediately and quickly threatened the viability of the restaurant.
>
> The existing customers who came for a quiet, high-service meal were unhappy to find more kids in the dining room, fewer menu choices to their liking, and far less service. Wait staff had to serve more tables to earn the same money. They weren't happy and a few of the better ones quit. Overall, business did not go up because the price per check went down even though the restaurant had more customers. And to make matters worse, the very profitable bar business went down. There was no way to go back, so the owner tried a third idea. The business was eventually sold.

> *The airline industry is a good example of positioning by price, ranging from low-cost, low-frills carriers such as Southwest to full-service airlines such as United and Delta. Passengers expect more from companies in the latter category.*

Part of your marketing strategy is understanding how pricing plays a part. Where you have positioned your company in comparison with your competitors' pricing says a great deal about the value of your product or service and the customers you are targeting. No company can serve a high-volume, price-sensitive market at the same time it serves a high-quality, high-service, upscale market that pays little concern to cost. You likely made the choice of what customer base you would seek at the time you started in business. It is almost impossible to change that strategy at this point.

Know Your Costs

The direct or variable costs of your product or service are what it costs to produce or provide each unit. This is critical information for you to have to base pricing decisions on, particularly in cases where the costs of material or labor go up and you must raise your prices to recapture those costs. Remember as well to include what is often a "hidden" cost of materials or products—the inventory that goes unsold and becomes a write-off. There are a number of reasons, ranging from style to spoilage: last year's fashions won't sell well this year or last week's soup must be disposed of. This must be added to your material cost.

For example, if you pay 50¢ for an item and sell it for a dollar, you may assume that your material costs are 50%. But if you dispose of 10% of your inventory unsold, after you include that cost your actual costs are 55%.

> *Before you make any drastic changes in pricing, be sure that any variation will improve the overall operation and bottom line.*

Set Gross Profit Targets

Based on your current revenue and your current overhead expense, you will know how close you are to acceptable levels of profitability. If you are selling $200,000 of goods and have indirect costs of $100,000, your gross profit margins must be in excess of 50%. Now you can determine whether you can increase those margins or you need to increase overall volume at current margins.

For example, increasing margins to 55% will give you a $10,000 profit cushion. Keeping margins and increasing sales to $220,000 will have about the same effect. You decide which goal is more achievable.

Remember the Competition

You are not likely to be alone in providing the goods and services you market. Customers always have a choice and often use a variety of criteria to make their decisions. So, as you look to make changes in your business that may include changes in your pricing structure, remember that you still must be competitive with other companies in similar businesses.

One of the considerations of how to move to a stronger pricing position is to redefine your company or your product in a way that makes you different from others. Customers will pay a premium for special handling or service.

The following are some areas you might consider that will allow for stronger pricing.

- Products that are hard to find elsewhere—special sizing, obsolete parts, small quantity, etc.
- Convenient location—a presence in an area where you're "the only game in town."
- Free delivery and in-home service in an industry where it is not the norm.
- Special credit terms—finance big purchases.
- Extended hours.
- Customized products.

If you are selling generic products in a traditional way,

Step one in profitable pricing is knowing your direct costs. Then you determine the percentage of markup.

> In the post-9/11 era, air travel dropped by 40%. Lower prices did not bring travelers back, but they increased the industry's red ink.

much of your pricing decisions will be made by market forces. Be different and it has an impact on your bottom line.

Lower Prices = Higher Sales?

Business is slow, revenues are down, and you need to do something to change that. Why not lower prices? Sales will go up, won't they?

It may surprise you to know that the answer is "Not necessarily." Depending on your product, it may be that if there is no demand prices won't create any. And discounting may jeopardize your financial health even further.

There are situations where short-term price incentives make sense. Selling last season's fashions or newly obsolete technology are two examples. Any money you get will make sense. But, in most cases, lowering prices would have to be followed by substantial growth in order not to affect your bottom line very seriously. You will likely be surprised to analyze how much in additional sales you require.

Here's an example. You have an item that sells for $500 and costs you $300. If you sell 100, you will gross $20,000 in profit.

100 units sold @ $500 =	$50,000
cost of $300 x 100 =	$30,000
gross profit =	$20,000

Let's assume you cut the price by 10% and sell at $450. Here's the new outcome.

100 units sold @ $450 =	$45,000
cost of $300 x 100 =	$30,000
gross profit =	$15,000

Your profit is now down by 25%, so you will have to sell 25% more items to produce the same gross profit dollars. That is a steep goal for a company trying to conserve resources.

Higher volume is likely to create a need for increased infrastructure as well—more space, more sales help, and even more administrative support. You may actually find yourself doing more for less.

What About a Price Increase?

If cutting prices isn't an easy solution, how about raising prices? In some instances, any movement—up or down—will attract the attention of your customers. If they see higher prices, they will check out your competition. In some cases, however, clients have developed strong patterns and habits that won't change that easily.

One of my clients was a restaurant, well known and highly regarded. The menu and prices had been in place for almost three years and the owner was reluctant to make changes. After serious consideration, a 5% across the board increase was put in place with a twist: the highest-priced item remained the same. Only two customers even mentioned the change and neither complained. The increase in profits made all the difference.

The effect of a price increase is the same as the effect of a cut: a small hike with a loss of volume will still provide the same profit dollars.

Here's an example:

100 units sold @ $500 = $50,000
cost of $300 x 100 = $30,000
gross profit = $20,000

A price increase of 10% and a 20% decrease in sales:

80 units sold @ $550 = $44,000
cost of $300 x 80 = $24,000
gross profit = $20,000

As in the case of higher volume, lower volume may

alter overhead costs because you will be handling, billing, and accounting for less. This may allow you to cut one or more positions. Less work for the same amount of profit.

The Fallacy of the Million-Dollar Business

Too many new business owners set their goals in terms of gross revenue numbers. The bigger the operation, the more successful it seems. But it is the bottom line that really matters—how much profit is generated to pay back investment as well as debt.

Growth for growth's sake is not the way to go. It is actually easier than you think. Charge prices that are lower than everybody else and you are bound to sell more than others and cash will flow until you run out. Losses are self-liquidating—the company will ultimately fail.

Find a pricing structure that allows for profits as well as growth.

Chapter Key Points

- Pricing strategies begin with your costs. Know what they are.
- Set targets for gross margins and try to keep them intact.
- Don't cut prices unless you have analyzed how much growth you will have to generate.
- Consider changing some of the elements of your product/service and increasing prices.
- Remember: it is the bottom line that matters.

CHAPTER 15

CREATE A FALLBACK POSITION—CRISIS MANAGEMENT

WHAT HAPPENS IF WORSE COMES TO WORST?

Tri-State Construction had done well for a number of years until a few of its school construction contracts went bad. Work slowed down because of other companies on the job and their men spent longer and cost more than they anticipated. The losses were even more damaging because of slow payments and funds that were retained until all sign-offs were complete.

First, suppliers weren't being paid and they called and complained and cut off credit. Then some tax payments and union contributions were missed and threats about levies and job actions escalated. The two men who owned the company put up some of their own money as their panic increased.

But it wasn't enough and the company lawyer recommended a Chapter 11 filing. Everyone was concerned about the impact on the company, but it wasn't that negative. Taxing bodies and the union knew they would be paid in full, so they allowed for time for work to be completed and money collected. Vendors weren't thrilled about taking a portion of what they were owed, but they wanted their customer to continue in business.

The process took less than six months and a stronger Tri-State Construction company emerged.

Once a business owner comes to grips with the seriousness of the deteriorating condition of the company, it's easy to think it's too late to do anything about it. And from time to time, that may be the case. However, what is truly amazing is how much you can still do to effect a turnaround at almost any point, even after years of losses and neglect. I have even had clients very late in bankruptcy reorganization, with 30 days remaining until a court-ordered liquidation, pull together a reorganization plan and save their business.

Consider a Worst-Case Scenario

You don't want to get that far, but you do want to think ahead and develop a contingency plan—plan B or even C. Your first goal is to cure the sick company and that's where you should focus your efforts. But if it can't be done, you'll also want to consider how to protect your personal assets from any creditors. You need to understand what a formal reorganization means and how to use it if necessary, either to extend the life of your business or to protect you and your business from the actions of creditors or discharge debts that can't be paid.

Learn the Basics About Bankruptcy

Until the early 1980s, the mere mention of the word "bankruptcy" struck fear in the hearts of most business owners. But in the 20 years since, a number of large public companies in retailing, heavy industry, and the airline industry have successfully reorganized under Chapter 11 bankruptcy and a good bit of the stigma has been eliminated.

It is not an easy task. I know. I took a small manufacturing company through that experience in the late 1980s

> *Tip* — Personally owned assets may be safe from business creditors if they are jointly owned. Ask your lawyer about these issues.

and we emerged still in business in 1990. In the past decade, I have worked on a number of reorganizations, including construction companies, a printing company, and a few restaurants. All but one came out successfully.

A large part of my consulting practice involves small companies that are experiencing difficulties that may put them on the brink of a filing. I know, from my own experience, that the longer any untreated problems are allowed to fester, the less likely the business is to recover or reorganize. If you have a growing instinct that you will need to use the bankruptcy laws to force creditors to settle debts at less than owed or to cancel a lease or contract, learn the rules now and plan well in advance.

You need to be speaking to professionals who deal regularly in bankruptcy to learn the various chapters (reorganization or liquidation) and what happens to a company involved in the process. It is never too early to consider your alternatives. I have known companies to plan as much as a year in advance to go through a Chapter 11 filing and restructure debt, terminate leases or contracts, or even vacate union agreements, all of which can be done in a bankruptcy reorganization.

Examining Different Types of Bankruptcy

There are various types of bankruptcy covered by the law. Chapter 12 is primarily for farms. Chapter 13, which is also referred to as the "wage earner's plan," is occasionally used when a small business is involved and the owner (or spouse) has a separate job. All debts are restructured based on personal income. However, the bankruptcy types most often used for business are the following:

- Chapter 11: Reorganization of debt that is usually

achieved by settling with creditors for less than full amount and paying over a period of time.
- Chapter 7: The liquidation of a business by selling all of the assets and paying creditors out of the proceeds. Also used in a personal liquidation.

How a Chapter 11 Reorganization Can Help You

The primary type of bankruptcy used for the purpose of business reorganization is a Chapter 11. You, as "debtor in possession," will be able to stay in charge of your business and you will have an initial 120 days as the exclusive party to file a plan describing how you expect to pay back your debts. You may get up to 90 days more by filing a request (motion) to the court. This time is meant to give you breathing space while you address the problems in your business, perhaps find new money, and ultimately work out a plan acceptable to creditors to pay back at least a portion of your debt. After the period of exclusivity has expired, any other party in interest (such as a creditor) may file a competing plan.

While the statistics are not very encouraging—only one company in four that files for Chapter 11 emerges as a going concern—that number has been increasing. And when you consider how seriously damaged most of the companies are that choose that course, perhaps it is remarkable that even 25% come out alive.

Chapter 11 reorganization is time-consuming and can be very costly. It is also possible to get the effect without going through the formal procedures. It is helpful to know what you can force on your creditors as terms, because you may be able to convince them to accept reduced or longer-term payments without the formal involvement of the court. The proceedings are costly to creditors as well.

Tip In a personal Chapter 7 filing, there are exemptions of property and assets that are kept by the debtor. Corporations or partnerships have no exemptions.

There are several areas where a Chapter 11 is very valuable. These are the terms you are likely to achieve in a plan and may be able to negotiate outside of the court.

Large Bank Debt, High Monthly Payment

Your bank loan is usually secured by the assets of your company and you must pay the bank back in full. If what you need is a longer term and lower monthly payments, a reorganization could work well for you. If you filed a plan that included extending a two-year loan to five years and paying the debt in full with interest, most courts would approve and your bank is unlikely to object. Try negotiating this directly with your bank.

You may also force the reduction of the amount of the loan if it is no longer secured by assets. Banks are sophisticated enough to know this, so an offer of payment in full is an incentive to negotiate.

Tax Debts and Forced Collection

The IRS can become relentless in collecting back taxes. Even if the IRS has levied your bank account, a bankruptcy filing will release those funds. A reorganization can give you up to six years to pay back taxes. You (or your attorney) can probably make a payment agreement without filing, but you are not likely to get more than two to three years. If you need more, a Chapter 11 may be necessary.

Vendor or Unsecured Debt

Many confirmed reorganization plans pay 25% or less of the outstanding unsecured debt, and that amount is paid over several years. These days, most large suppliers understand this reality. You may be able to voluntarily offer 50¢ on the dollar over a year or two and wipe out a large debt to suppliers. Have your attorney make these calls if you are uncomfortable.

Perhaps the biggest value of a Chapter 11 filing is the imposition of what is known as the "automatic stay." All creditors, including the IRS, must cease any action they have been pursuing. If you have been spending your time and energy fighting off lawsuits and taking angry calls rather than working on the operation of your company, this will now change. Actions can still continue, but they will proceed more slowly and have to go to the court first. This will give you the time you need to increase profitability and cash flow so you can repay debts.

Tip — A company can also be sold in a Chapter 11 reorganization. The new owner arranges to pay the reduced and restructured debt.

The Basics of Chapter 7 Bankruptcy

The other primary type of bankruptcy is a Chapter 7 liquidation. When a company no longer has any hope of reorganization, this is how it often ends up.

At this point, the entire business (which is usually but not always closed) is turned over to the court, which appoints a trustee to sell the assets and pay debts according to a prescribed formula. If all assets are pledged to the bank, the bank takes control and conducts the sale. After the secured debt is paid, the following are then paid.

Administrative Fees

These are primarily legal fees. It should not surprise you to know that the more funds available, the higher these benefits will become, perhaps because they have to be collected and administered.

Priority Tax Claims

These claims constitute the company's outstanding debt to any and all taxing authorities. They must be paid in full before any unsecured debt can be paid. This category also includes wages owed and union fees.

Unsecured Debt

If there are any funds left, they are distributed on a pro rata basis to trade creditors or others that have unsecured claims.

Other Options to Examine

There are other choices, even for an insolvent company. You can file a Chapter 11 and then, after a few months of planning a strategy, file a liquidating plan. That means that, instead of a plan of reorganization, you will file documents with the court that state how your assets will be sold and how the money will be applied to retire secured debt and then any residual to unsecured debt.

The downside of a Chapter 11 is that the legal fees charged to you in advance of the filing are much higher than in a Chapter 7 and most of the Chapter 7 fees are paid from the proceeds of the liquidation. In addition, the Chapter 11 will be directed by you and require you to continue to work. A filing of a Chapter 7 immediately gets you out of the business and a trustee takes over the assets. If you have a new job or new project to pursue, this gets you there faster.

However, trustees do not work quickly; they have little incentive to do so. If your assets are housed in a rented building, months could go by before a sale is conducted; all the rent will be deducted from the proceeds. The longer a trustee keeps a case going, the more his or her fees add up; these too are drawn from the sale. The effect of this is to seriously diminish the amount that is applied to your debts. In addition, you know far more than a trustee about where to sell your assets for the highest return and you will most likely achieve a better result with lower costs. The key to decision making here is your personal situation at the time and the level of individual liability you are trying to reduce.

Determine Whether Your Company Is Solvent

It is a difficult task to determine the value of a small business. As a going concern, it has the value of its profits and the intangibles such as goodwill and market share in addition to the net asset value. An orderly liquidation might bring the cost value of inventory and less than top resale value of machinery and equipment. At this point, most goodwill and other intangibles have less worth, but the name and current accounts may be salable. A forced liquidation of your assets will bring in only pennies on the dollar, and most small businesses are not solvent if forced into such a sale.

At this difficult time, you must determine the solvency of your company because it will be incorporated into your strategy. Can you sell the company as a going concern? If you did, would the sale price be sufficient to retire all outstanding secured debt? While most owners have full intention of paying trade creditors, in most cases those debts are unsecured and you cannot be held personally liable for them, particularly if your company has been operating as a corporation. That status has protected you personally. (Again, we're looking at worst-case scenarios and trying to protect you and your personal assets.)

The second test of solvency would be a look at the value of tangible assets—including property, machinery, equipment, and inventory—sold in an orderly fashion over time. Would this type of sale realize enough cash to retire debt? If it would be close, could you perhaps sell the name or accounts for an amount sufficient to satisfy creditors? If the answer is yes, you are still in the area of a solvent business. A good test of solvency would be to draw a balance sheet of sale values of your assets and see what the net worth would be if you conducted the sale. This is shown in Figure 15-1.

Assets	
Cash	(In banks)
Accounts Receivable	(Those that are collectable)
Machinery and Equipment	(Resale value)
Inventory	(Current sale value)
Total	_____

Liabilities	
Loans	(Current balance)
Accounts Payable	(Total due)
Outstanding wages and taxes due	(Consider penalties and interest)
Total	_____

FIGURE 15-1. Balance sheet based on liquidation of assets

The difference between assets and liabilities is net liquidation value or, if a deficit, your potential exposure.

As mentioned before, few companies, large or small, can withstand a distressed liquidation. Even if your property has real value, most buyers hold back because they expect major bargains at this type of sale. There are so many stops along the way to save value that it is a real mistake to allow your business to get to this point. It's all dependent on when you come to terms with your problem and whether or not you begin to take action to turn the situation around.

A Solvent Company Can Be Sold

The problems that have brought you to your knees can be just the challenge someone else seeks. A new owner may be able to bring in fresh capital that surely will help. New equity can be an incentive to your bank to renegotiate loans and vendors may be willing to grant more credit than you were able to get. It may not seem fair, but it does have a value to you. If you are no longer able to turn the company around, you want to get out with your own assets intact and perhaps some cash to start over again.

If you find a buyer who pays you and assumes the company debts as well, you will be free to do just that. There are several ways to set up a deal—a sale of the business intact as a going concern or just a sale of the assets. There are pros and cons to each, so good legal and accounting advice is absolutely essential.

I would caution you on two issues.

The first is accepting a payout or a consulting fee for part of the purchase price. Forget the tax implications, unless they are monumental. Think about how you will feel about being almost a partner to the new buyer. What can you do if the money isn't forthcoming? If the company you are selling has been a borderline performer, your buyer will often have the same cash problems you did. Can you afford a lawyer to fight for you if you don't get paid? In the worst cases, the new owner ends up going into bankruptcy owing the former owner much of the purchase price. These cases are more prevalent than you think. I personally know of five and none has ended beneficially for the original owner. If you have the choice, take a little less and take it in cash.

The second issue is the signing of any agreement that requires you not to compete. You have been working in the industry or type of business you are the most familiar with, so not being able to work in the field may be more of a problem than you believe. Unless you've always wanted to go off and become an artist, don't agree to walk away from your knowledge and your business relationships without serious consideration.

Even an Insolvent Business Can Be Sold

You may have old equipment, out-of-date inventory, and debts to the sky, but you also have a name, a share of your market, and other intangible assets that may be of great value to another company in the industry. Do you have a contract or a longstanding relationship with a customer that one of your competitors is just drooling over? How about finding out what that would be worth to that competitor? Explore how the two of you could put together a deal that would get you something even for a very troubled business.

Or is there a company in an allied business that could make a success out of an expansion in your industry? One example that I am familiar with is a janitorial supply company that expanded into safety and became a real regional player by purchasing small troubled distributors and selling extra products to their existing customers, making a turnaround happen fairly quickly. They paid very little and enjoyed a substantial return.

Make a Plan in Advance—Always Good Advice

The more you find yourself driven by circumstance, the worse off you will be. It is good advice to have a plan when you are starting out, good advice to update it, and good

> *You believed in your business enough to start it or take it over. Wouldn't it be nice to see it continue on? Selling it may offer that chance.*

advice to create a plan to end your company or transfer it to someone else. Review what has been described in this chapter and determine where your company really is at this time. Choose a course of action; determine who will handle all the details and exactly what your time line will be. Write it all down and review it after a day or two to make sure you really are doing what is necessary and what you want to do. Then set the plan in motion.

One of my current clients has just made some serious decisions on how we will operate over the next three months. His most obvious problem is serious cash flow problems created by several large customers who have refused to pay their outstanding bills. We also want to monitor his overall profitability. Our strategy is as follows:

1. Turn delinquent unpaid receivables over to attorney for collection.
2. Contact suppliers to secure more time to pay bills.
3. Put a small amount of additional working capital into business.
4. Determine if company can make enough profit to pay debts if we are not paid.
5. Using the results and information from the first four steps, we will decide whether a Chapter 11 may be a possibility.

A Good Attorney Is Essential

At this point in the life of your business, you need the help of a knowledgeable business attorney, preferably one with a substantial amount of bankruptcy experience. Don't hire someone who does not come highly recommended and don't let the attorney's fee be the deciding factor. The level of skill and the level of cooperation between you and your counsel can make an enormous difference in the outcome of your case. Almost all successful reorganizations are directed by experienced lawyers, and even the best outcome with a liquidation requires legal expertise. In both reorganization and liquidation, there will be opposing forces: your lawyer must be attentive to what's happening in the case and respond effectively. I have taken on a few clients after their cases were jeopardized by a borderline attorney and their situation usually had deteriorated seriously and left few options. Property that could have been saved has been confiscated and pressure is coming from all sides.

An inexperienced bankruptcy lawyer will get eaten up alive by the system, more astute opposing counsel, and often the judges themselves, who have little patience for cases that drag on without reason and aren't well handled. Make a thoughtful choice in the beginning. Ask someone who has been through it or go to the court and observe lawyers in action to find one who seems talented. Don't take a risk at this stage.

At this point, it all may be a bit overwhelming. First, you've been worn down by your problems, and now your choice seems to be between bad and worse. Try to keep in mind that it won't last forever and there will be new opportunities and horizons when that day comes. I know—I've been there ... and I've seen others on both sides of the nightmare as well. Sometimes, the recovery is to an opportunity for better than the business that got into trouble. Life does go on.

Chapter Key Points

- Consider a Chapter 11 bankruptcy reorganization by learning the rules and finding good counsel.
- Determine the solvency of the company by drawing a balance sheet based on liquidation values.

- If you sell the business as a going concern, be cautious about how you will be paid.
- If you cannot sell the whole business, sell the pieces to your competitors or to an allied business.
- Conduct an orderly liquidation of all assets to get top value and retire debts.

CHAPTER 16

DEVELOP A BEST-CASE SCENARIO

IT'S GOING TO WORK OUT OK

> Wayne had a growing real estate company acquiring and managing properties as well as marketing them. After a tough winter when he was hit with enormous utility bills and higher than anticipated repairs, Wayne was concerned about planning for his future. He wondered if he should sell off his properties to pay debt.
>
> An analysis of his financials showed that while cash flow might be temporarily tough, equity was solid and growing due to increasing values of property. The decision was made not to do any panic selling but to increase property transactions instead.
>
> Purchasing and managing additional properties provided increased operating revenues to cover overhead. Breakeven was achieved fairly soon and the goal of positive cash was reached in just over six months.
>
> There are times when it looks tough, yet good times are within sight if you can create the vision.

It's OK to Be Optimistic

You must protect yourself from developing a siege mentality about your current crisis. While it has been critical to face the reality about your current problems, you must also understand that the condition of your business will improve. The steps you are taking now will make you stronger and any turnaround in the general economy or in your industry will enhance your efforts. You must think about (and plan for) an optimistic future so that you will be prepared for new opportunities when they arise. You don't want to allow yourself to become immobilized and stay in your current crisis longer than necessary.

If this is the first time your business has become stagnant or experienced a downturn in revenues, you'll need to look around for new ways to create positive energy for the thrust forward, even while you are stabilizing your current operation. Here are six key points to remember.

1. Don't liquidate valuable inventory or needed equipment for cash.
2. Set new benchmarks for your company that assume you will make a recovery.
3. Create a plan to achieve your new goals.
4. Communicate and sell these goals to employees, customers, and vendors. These people are critical to success.
5. Spend some time looking at future trends.
6. Keep on developing new (and better) customers.

Don't Cannibalize Inventory or Equipment to Raise Cash

If a recession has softened the demand for your products and you are using only a portion of your capacity, don't let the unused part go to seed. But be careful in deciding what to sell. Your best equipment or most marketable inventory will likely be the easiest to liquidate, but may be almost the toughest to replace when you need to move forward. It may be tempting to relieve the pressure for cash by selling valuable assets, but it is imprudent to do it.

One of my clients was in a cash crunch and was being denied shipments of some of his important product lines because of credit problems. In order to raise cash, he sold off other very marketable inventory below his cost. This was a desperate attempt to raise funds to release the needed products. Then, when business improved and he went to replace inventory he had liquidated, these suppliers also denied credit. All that was left to sell was out of date and undesirable. His company never had a chance to come back. When the second set of suppliers cut him off, his company was all but dead.

Establish and Set New Goals

Go back to your early days in business when you were projecting how you would grow and what your sales and profits would be like in three or five years. Even if they haven't stopped falling, find a base and build new numbers from there. While you may have used double-digit growth numbers in your original plans, now is the time to be conservative. Assume a growth pattern in line with overall economic growth and, if you are developing a new product, service, or customer base, adjust your numbers on that basis. An increase that exceeds inflation will offer some additional profits. That's the direction you want to go.

Now you have established new numbers that are derived from your current circumstance and these should be realistic targets to hit. Share them with those in your organization responsible for the effort it will take to achieve these goals. Perhaps you can make it into a contest, with small prizes or plaques for those who achieve their own portions.

Create a Plan to Reach Your Goals

Don't use the current downturn as an excuse not to create a plan to reach the goal of prosperity. Once you have decided how you may be able to achieve some new success, decide on a step-by-step plan to get there. Then write the steps down in the form of a new business plan. How will you find the new sales that you will need to move forward? Who are the customers and how do you expect to reach them?

If you are planning on offering a new product or service, describe it fully, working out all the bugs on paper rather than by trial and error. What is the potential for this innovation and, again, how will you reach the market to introduce it?

It is very difficult to convince a small business owner to create a new business plan after he or she is already operating the business, but if you are looking for an effective way to cast your eye toward the future, you should consider this exercise. It also is a good project to undertake in the late night hours when you aren't able to sleep. As you accomplish the steps, your confidence will rise.

Share Your Optimism with Employees, Vendors, and Customers

Having new plans on the drawing board is a good way to inspire those stressed out by current difficulties to look to the future optimistically. If you seem to be conducting a constant disaster drill, new problems may crop up that

Tip The aging of baby boomers is one example of new opportunity. Products and services that meet their growing needs will prosper in the next decade.

weren't even on the horizon when you began trying to turn the company around.

For example, one industrial distributor I worked with briefly became so obsessed with his excess inventory and selling it to raise cash (which was an important issue) that his entire sales staff focused on this issue. In the meantime, other distributors were calling on my client's customers with new products and new marketing ideas. I learned after the fact that by the time he had raised most of the money from his inventory liquidation, one of his best salesmen had quit and the entire company was demoralized. He won the battle but lost the war.

Your employees need to see the future and, as important, to feel that they will have a contribution in it. Your vendors who may be making accommodations now should feel that there will be a payoff for their efforts down the road. And your customers will be less inclined to find new vendors if they see that you will be around to continue to service their needs.

Don't be unrealistically optimistic and don't promise an instant fix, but do make it clear the energy and effort are being directed at a future you believe will be better.

Stay Aware of the Trends That Will Affect Your Company

Many entrepreneurs are real visionaries, seeing opportunities that others miss and creating entire businesses around them. Even if you haven't based your success on cutting-edge technology or new marketing opportunities, it is still dangerous to become so involved in day-to-day operations that you exclude any and all future trends. This is true whether you are involved in a turnaround or not. And now is no exception.

Tip — Trying out new products for future release is a way to change the tone from current struggles to potential opportunities.

What seemed futuristic only a few years ago is becoming today's reality. The way goods are produced, sold, and distributed has undergone major change and continues to change. You should spend some time learning about and thinking about these developments. You may come across an innovation that could improve your operation enough to accelerate your turnaround. Don't stop thinking about tomorrow.

The Internet and e-commerce are the major change of the last decade. It has helped most companies but has hurt some as well. Spending an enormous amount of money on a Web presence and assuming that large sales volume will be made on those sites has destroyed more than a few players. Perhaps this has been your story as well.

> While the Web has not yet lived up to all the hype about huge sales, it does play an important new role in exchange of funds as well as information. Money moves faster when it is transferred electronically.

Nevertheless, do not stop learning and exploring the new possibilities. You may be able to order directly from your suppliers and even check their inventory to see what delivery times will be. You may find sites that offer collective purchasing or comparative information. And your own company Web site is a good marketing tool to increase sales.

Continue to Develop New Customers

In the normal life of any business, customers go and customers come. Whether you plan for it or not, it is bound to happen. When your business is in a growth phase, you will be out actively seeking new customers. Eventually, those efforts slow down and the time when you need new customers the most—when business is tough—is often when your effort is stopped. Don't let that happen: you need to remain active in the market.

Problem solving, particularly at the level where you are at present, is time-consuming and energy-draining work, and it's tough to be able to muster the enthusiasm to see new prospects or to motivate your sales force to do it. But if you don't forge ahead in new customer calls, your business will continue to shrink by attrition and then, when everything begins to turn your way, the growth you desire will be more difficult to find. Keeping up with sales and marketing now is a valuable course of action.

And there is a side benefit to this effort. Most of us are very proud of the businesses we have built, regardless of the current difficulties. Having a chance to go out and tell our stories to new prospects is a reaffirmation of our achievements and can actually help to rebuild our own confidence. So go out and see new people—it's good for your business and it's good for you.

Chapter Key Points

- If you plan only for the worst, you may create your own reality. If you plan for the best, you'll be prepared to seize on any opportunity. Develop a plan for the best-case scenario.

- Keep assets intact to take advantage of better opportunities.

- Set new goals for your company that show forward progress.

- Make sure all stakeholders (employees, vendors, and customers) understand that you are planning for the future.

- Always keep open to new trends and continue to develop new customers.

SECTION IV

▲ ▲ ▲

IMPLEMENT THE TURNAROUND

CHAPTER 17

THE VALUE OF OUTSIDE CONSULTANTS

REACH FOR A HELPING HAND

Many entrepreneurs are specialists in one of the aspects of their business. If that describes you and the thought of doing all this analysis, making tough decisions, and implementing the changes is more than you want to undertake, there is help. You can find an outside consultant to add independent objectivity to any or all of the following tasks you need to accomplish.

Identifying the Problems

Entrepreneurs often are so involved with day-to-day operation of the business that drawing back to get an objective view becomes difficult. If you have devoted time in the technical or marketing area of your operation and put together a team of managers and employees to complete other tasks, you may no longer have a good overview of these areas. However, because of changes in the business environment around you, an area that is most unfamiliar to you may be exactly where serious changes must be made. You are very astute if you understand how to complete a totally objective analysis of how costs can be cut or improvements can be made.

Very few entrepreneurs are specialists in all areas of business from marketing to production to finances. Often, there is one area of interest and

> **Areas for Consulting Advice**
> - Determining the problem areas.
> - Setting new priorities.
> - Developing a strategy.
> - Implementing a plan.

skill that is the driving force for starting a business and, if a strong team isn't formed to handle the other aspects of operations, many of the problems develop in those areas. It is quite difficult for the owner who has little interest in finance to review his own performance in that area or for a contractor who loves to work outside and build to make a serious analysis of his company's marketing strategy. In fact, the company may not even have one. This is clearly a case where outside advice can be of great value.

Setting Priorities and Developing a Strategy

Once you know what areas require attention, you will have to establish your priorities and determine how you will implement any needed changes. Some of the work required may be time- and energy-consuming, and this may be difficult for you to accomplish at the same time you are completing your day-to-day work.

The instinct of any business owner is to plan for an immediate turnaround. You may have been dealing with your difficulties for many months or even years, and now you want them to be over quickly. Setting reasonable priorities and timelines as well as the strategy to accomplish your plan may be beyond the stress and impatience level that you are currently feeling. The assistance of an outsider in this phase may help you set more reasonable goals and timelines.

Implementing the Plan

The last phase of your turnaround will be the implementation of your plan for change. This phase may involve selling off assets, calling creditors, closing unprofitable operations, laying off employees, increasing prices, collecting past due accounts from customers, or changing vendors. Some of these tasks can be very cumbersome from a personal perspective; if you attempt them alone, you may end up putting them off longer than you should.

Many times when change is brought to an organization as a result of difficulties, everyone—including the owner—experiences feelings of guilt, frustration, and even outright anger. Finger pointing can happen, with employees believing that the owner made all the mistakes and the owner feeling that no one in his employ cares as much as he does. The truth, of course, is that most likely both have done some things quite well and both have made some mistakes. Everyone can feel the stress and an outsider may be able to take the brunt of it and keep those who are working together from confronting each other. This can be particularly true when a business involves a married couple or a family. The value of outside help is in moving forward into the implementation rather than trying to relive what went wrong.

These are very good reasons to hire an outside consultant to work with you. Once you have made the decision, where do you find the best consultant for your operation and how much will it cost? These two issues are connected because there are places to find very low or actually no-cost advisors and there are consultants who charge a fairly high rate usually comparable to a lawyer's fee. Your goal is to balance the two and find someone who is cost-effective.

> *There are a variety of good sources to consider for help:*
> *1. Local colleges or universities*
> *2. Local and federal development agencies*
> *3. Private consultants*

Finding Help at Universities

You may be able to find undergraduate business students or even MBA candidates to do work for you at no cost. I have worked with both and found great value in their projects. Needless to say, the MBA students are more astute and can tackle more complex problems. The downside of using students is that they need a certain amount of supervision, but the upside is that the energy and enthusiasm of a student can be infectious.

If you can find a student who wishes to use your company for case study for part of his or her MBA requirements, you may really hit the jackpot. The project may last three to five months and it is the equivalent of having a highly motivated and valuable unpaid employee. The most critical aspect for you will be to agree on exactly what work should be accomplished and for you to give your intern the time and attention as well as complete data to make the job worthwhile.

Also available at selected universities are Small Business Development Centers funded by the Small Business Administration as well as the states, foundations, and institutions themselves. Operated by faculty members and hired professionals, each offers a variety of programs and courses and one-on-one counseling. The services will be free or low-cost, but the work is meant to be short-term. For longer projects, you will have to look elsewhere. But if you are looking for some feedback on decisions you are considering or if you know where the trouble is and want someone to give you technical advice, this may be the right place. Check the Web site: www.sba.gov/sbdc.

Getting Help from Public Agencies

The SBA also funds a counseling program called SCORE (Service Corps of Retired Executives), www.score.org, which offers free help to any business owner who requests it. The volunteers have retired from business careers and are willing to work with small business owners as long as they are needed. A word of caution here is that not all the volunteers are equally qualified. If you are assigned a counselor who you feel doesn't have anything of substance to contribute, you will have to terminate the relationship. If the thought of having to "fire" a volunteer makes you uncomfortable, this may not be the program for you.

Another place to find free assistance is the development authority in your city or, in some instances, your local neighborhoods. Many of these quasi-government agencies have business development specialists who can help with technical assistance or referrals and may even be able to assist you with loan programs that you could not access on your own.

Start with your city agency and ask if they have technical assistance programs for small business owners. They may refer you to a development group in your community. If you are interested in moving your business (perhaps to save some money), call the agency in the community you are considering. You will be pleasantly surprised to learn how enthusiastic they are to attract new jobs to their neighborhood. Few of these agencies have actual loan funds available, but they can help you put together a package to find loans from a variety of sources.

If you are a woman or a member of a minority group, there may be a special agency or association whose main purpose is to work with nontraditional business owners. Check your local phone book or call the minority enterprise office of your state or the regional SBA office (www.sba.gov/regions/states.html).

Using Private Consultants

Here the costs jump dramatically, as private consultants charge by the hour and fees can run anywhere from $75 to $175 per hour. There is no shortage of business consultants available at this time, since many former corporate managers who have found themselves separated from their previous jobs have started independent consulting practices. Their backgrounds can be very different and not all consultants are equal. A good advisor can be worth far more than what he or she may charge, but the burden is on you to take the time to choose carefully. And it will also be your job to set the task, make sure time isn't wasted, and pay attention to billable hours as they mount.

How to Choose a Good Consultant

This is an important decision and you should take the time to make it carefully. Don't hire the first person who walks into your office claiming to be a consultant, even if he or she makes a good impression. Talk to at least three candidates and solicit general business ideas as well as specific information about them and their backgrounds. You should feel free to discuss the problems of your company on a general basis and get a sense of what type of problem solving each candidate offers.

Conducting an Interview with a Consultant

The first thing to note in an interview with any professional is how the two of you hit it off. You will be working very closely together in a situation that can be at times relatively stressful, so a cordial relationship and mutual respect are important.

You will also find that most consultants present themselves with a variety of written material, although few will have anything that resembles a typical résumé. You still want to know about the individual you will be working with and not just about his or her firm. There are national companies that will send two, three, or four consultants to do a single project. I am frankly skeptical about that procedure. First, I believe it is more costly, because each one will have to come up to speed about your operation before he or she can be of real help. Second, because each individual will have his or her own level of expertise, the work may be inconsistent.

You have the right to meet with the consultant assigned to your case, face to face, in advance of agreeing to hire any firm. If a national or even a local consulting practice is not willing to agree to this practice, I would suggest that you pass on the offer. A sole practitioner will allow you to accomplish this, but he or she may not have expertise in all the areas you require. A small, local practice may be an effective alternative. Figure 17-1 is a checklist to use when interviewing a consultant.

---

1. **What is his or her personal background?**
   Small business or corporate
   Specialized or general business
   Middle manager or the "one in charge"
   Any entrepreneurial experience
2. **How much consulting experience?**
   What types of projects
   What specific results achieved
   What types of businesses
3. **What is his or her general business philosophy?**
   View of current business environment
   View of business goals/personal goals
4. **What reference can he or she give about himself or herself, not just his or her firm?**

FIGURE 17-1. Consultant interview checklist

Check References Carefully

You should call every name given to you as a reference by any consultant and ask the reference a series of detailed questions. You should not expect other business owners to give you confidential information about their companies and the work they had done, but you should expect to hear general comments. If more than one of the references on your list seem hesitant to talk, this should be a warning sign. Some of the questions to ask include the following:

1. Was the work satisfactory?
2. Did the consultant relate well to managers and employees?
3. Was the project (or series of tasks) completed on time?
4. Was the original estimate accurate?
5. Were there many add-ons (items not covered by the original scope of the work but necessary)?

This last item is critical because it may indicate that the consultant consciously bids a job with a low estimate and then runs up the tab (and the time required). Variances between the estimate and the actual cost happen, but they should not be a pattern.

One way to investigate further is to ask references if they know of any other clients who have worked with the consultant. You can expect to get only the names of the most satisfied client from your candidate, but you may be able to uncover other information by doing additional research.

How to Work Successfully with a Consultant

Any time you hire a professional, you should negotiate to

> *Don't look at the retainer or "up-front" costs as the determining factor. It is the final cost that matters.*

agreement the terms of your work together. This is true for lawyers and accountants and particularly true for consultants. You would never hire an employee to do an unspecified job during an uncontrolled period of time for a fee still undetermined. You must have a clear understanding with your consultant as to the following:

1. The scope of the work
2. The length of the assignment
3. The approximate cost

Narrow the Scope to Manageable Goals

If you hire a consultant to do a complete turnaround of your company, you are talking about some very substantial expense. For a business in the $2-$5 million range, this type of work could cost $30,000 to $100,000. You could expect to have someone with you on a full-time basis for a month or so and then fairly regularly after that. It is not my contention that this is not a valuable way to handle your problem because it is. There are a number of talented turnaround experts who can be of substantial value to your company. But my experience has been that few companies experiencing difficulties can afford this level of assistance.

If keeping the cost down is critical to you, then good control of your consultant starts with the scope of the job. If you are feeling that you have no clue, why not begin with an analysis of your operation that will become a report with specific recommendations?

This type of assignment is short term and the consultant should quote you an absolute time and cost for this work. Depending on the complexity of your business, the work should take two to five days and cost $3,000 to $10,000. Most consultants who work with small businesses would be willing to complete this type of analysis.

Tip Lawyers now use a "letter of engagement" to clarify their agreement with a client. Ask your consultant for one as well.

Beyond this phase, the work should be specifically identified by the area to be covered and the goal of the task. Open-ended assignments can go on forever without any meaningful conclusion or result to determine their success. You don't want to become dependent on your consultant. Setting goals, even if they are interim goals, will allow you to analyze how the work is progressing.

Set Time Frames for Completion

When someone is doing a job that is unfamiliar to you, it is hard to assess how long it will take to complete the work. That doesn't mean that you should allow a consultant to finish at his or her own pace.

If your car was in a garage for repairs, you would want to know when the mechanic would finish them and you would ask that question when you dropped off the vehicle at the garage. Before you allow a consultant to tinker with your business, ask him or her to set a specific time for completion as well as a date for submitting a report. If it is a long-term project, you should have dates for completion of phases along the way.

Time Is Money: Set a Price

Once you have determined the scope of the work and a specific time to accomplish the task, your consultant will make an estimate of the required hours. Virtually all professionals charge by the hour, so you will now have at least a close estimate of the cost of the project. You may want to allow a range, such as 25 to 30 hours, so that additional tasks can be added if needed. However, before you begin, you should have a firm idea of the total cost of your project.

Put Your Agreement in Writing

Some consultants use a contract to establish the terms of their work. The only problem I have with this is that you will have to add the cost of a legal review before you sign. Make sure that it includes a cancellation clause based on items within your control, such as performance, and also that there is no fee escalation clause in case of termination.

What I prefer is a letter of understanding or a proposal covering the items I have discussed: scope, time, and cost. This should also specify a cancellation policy.

Chapter Key Points

- The responsibility for the turnaround of your company is yours, but it can be very beneficial to find outside assistance.
- Determine the project that requires help.
- Consider free help as well as paid professionals.
- Be careful about choosing a consultant; interview more than one candidate.
- Learn about the individual consultant who will be doing the work, not just the firm he or she represents.
- Check references.
- Negotiate the scope, time, and cost of the project.

CHAPTER 18

EMPLOYEES—OPTIONS

PEOPLE ARE YOUR BUSINESS

> With all the press around the large bankruptcy filings of Kmart and Enron and WorldCom, some of the most controversial coverage surrounded large retention bonuses paid to the executive who stayed after many were laid off. The court and legal professionals who work regularly in the field of restructuring understand that it takes talent to lead and inspire a successful reorganization. Retention of those with the right skills is an important goal.
>
> In fact, a talented "turnaround" person can provide the key skills that may make the difference in how a company sails through these unchartered waters.

US Airways filed for Chapter 11 almost immediately after hiring David Siegel, an experienced manager with troubled airlines. He turned hostile employee relationships around and secured the cost cutting agreements that were critical and would never have been given to his predecessor.

There is bound to be a change of personnel during a business turnaround: initially, you may be cutting back on staff; later in the game, people may leave to pursue other jobs. This won't be easy and at times it's hard not to have feelings that those who leave are disloyal. But try to put yourself in their shoes and be sympathetic. There is no doubt that the stress level has gotten high and there is likely to be general concern about the future. If employees can find positions with more security, don't be surprised if they take them.

Keeping Key Employees

All of the advice to this point has been to watch expenses and cut where possible. At the same time, you don't want to allow things to deteriorate—and they will if many of your key people start to jump ship. Now may be the time to invest some of your savings in keeping people motivated. It may surprise you to know that, even in bankruptcy, retention bonuses are an accepted practice. Perhaps you need to consider this technique.

A bonus that is tied to longevity goes something like this. An amount is chosen that is reasonable, given current circumstances. Part of that is paid on signing; the rest is paid incrementally over a number of years only if the employee stays with the company. The bonus may be increased by any financial recovery or may include an equity position in the company, in return for good results.

Information may also serve as an incentive. Not knowing what is going on can make people more fearful than

SECOND WIND

> *Tip* — Not every employee is critical to your business and its future. Don't mix personal loyalties with good business sense. But do be aware that you have a team and the key players have value. Keep them if you can.

they might otherwise be. Be honest about how serious the problems are, but give as much assurance as is honest on what is in place to correct the trouble. Make this the ongoing policy.

Consider Using Subcontractors

You may have been doing all of the work in house so that you could maintain the control. By now you likely have realized that productivity is the key to profits. Every employee must have work output commensurate with his or her compensation. Few businesses can afford having employees stand around.

The question you must ask yourself before doing any serious hiring is "Can we outsource this work and save money?"

For example, you have always offered free delivery of the merchandise that you sell. Over the years, you had two trucks and drivers on the road. Now, the lower level of business means neither delivery routes is busy enough to pay its expense. One driver leaves. Do you replace him?

Before deciding to hire, why not check out delivery services? Can you outsource package delivery to a vendor who will save you money? The cost per package is one consideration, but remember the total cost of a driver, including benefits, and the cost of the truck, its maintenance, depreciation, and insurance. This may be the way to go until you get busy enough to fully utilize another in-house person or it may be a permanent solution. And in doing the analysis around this decision, perhaps you will discover that you need to add a surcharge for this service.

There are administrative services available on outsourcing as well as subcontracting out some of your manufacturing operations or warehousing. Why not let a specialized company do the work it's best suited for and you can focus on your special talents? Remember: it isn't the revenues, it's the profits.

Part-Time Workers May Be Enough

In the past decade, more and more workers have come to accept part-time employment—some because they want it and others because that is what is available. That may be a solution for your staffing needs. People who take care of parents or young children, those going back to school for additional education, the semi-retired, and even those wanting time to start their own businesses are all candidates. In some cases, the flexible schedule is a motivator.

These part-time employees may stay long term and make a big contribution to your company. So don't think of this as a fill-in solution; it may be sufficient to get the work done and keep the overall costs in line.

Do You Know About Employee Leasing?

I am sure most business owners are aware of temporary employment firms. You use their workers for a short-term engagement and they charge you a premium hourly rate. It is a solution for a very busy time, vacation fill-ins, or the early stages of growth. But it can be expensive and not good for the long haul.

There is another alternative you could explore—*employee leasing*. Not only is this a way to find new employees, but it is even possible to move current employees to the leasing company and have them continue their work on a different basis.

There are benefits to you. It will end the need for all payroll maintenance. The leasing company withholds and pays all taxes. In some instances, such as unemployment taxes, its rate will be lower than yours, so it will save you money. And because the leasing company has many more employees than you, it may be able to provide more in the way of benefits such as insurance and pension plans at an overall lower cost. This is something you may want to learn about.

Hiring New Workers

The time comes when there is too much to do and a key slot needs to be filled. Chances are that by trying to wait long enough, you may have actually waited a bit too much. Now the panic begins to find someone. But don't be hasty. Don't throw any warm body at an open desk.

Remember the time and the cost of training any new employee. Regardless of the skill set the hire brings to the job, he or she is unlikely to be productive for weeks at least, if not months. This really puts pressure on the company to absorb the workload, do the training, and not add to the expenses. Bottom line is that the choice is critical: take time and do it right.

Before Making the Offer

In addition to accepting résumés, you want to have a formal application as well. Résumés are designed to put the best spin on all the attributes of the applicant. Ask more in-depth questions. Inquire about *all* of the jobs held in the past five years. Find out if the candidate has jumped from one to another. Ask for the names of immediate supervisors; you may want to speak to them if there are any questions or if the job is critical enough. Include items specific

> *The interview is important—don't just gloss over it, being pleasant. If you are not comfortable at the task, invite someone else in the organization to join you. And one or both of you should write down the questions you intend to ask.*

to your company or industry.

And always, *always* check references. The ones listed on the résumé are likely to say good things, so you may also need to call former employers. These days they may not be as candid as they would like, fearing some legal reprisal. Perhaps their reluctance to say much will be an indication that further investigation is needed.

I once helped a client hire an office manager. Although her skills seemed more than what we needed, we both had some mixed feelings during the interview. I called a former employer and he declined to say anything beyond the fact that she had worked there. I should have taken that a warning, but I didn't. It was a disaster—one that we could have prevented.

In short order, this new employee had turned the office into chaos. She changed files and systems to suit herself and to prevent others from accessing them. This was her own form of job security, she thought. It meant that all work had to be moved past her, taking time and causing poor information flow. We needed someone on this job and, in our haste, we lost three months and had to start all over again.

Take Time to Train

People who start businesses don't have the luxury of training on the job: it is all learn-by-doing. So it is easy for us to forget that others are at a loss when they join the company. Few small businesses have the resources to create and implement a formal training program. Managers explain as they go along, hoping that eventually the new employee will get up to speed.

Sometimes it happens that way, but most times this method takes longer. Instead, try writing down all the responsibilities of the job and then breaking them down into tasks with as many details as possible. On the first or second go-around, make sure someone knowledgeable is there to answer any questions and explain the shortcuts and the potential problems. Don't ever let someone learn by error: they may make a serious one along the way.

During difficult times, a company often shrinks in both revenue and number of employees. When growth begins again, new people will be needed. The timing and the method you use will be critical to your success.

Chapter Key Points

- Always make an effort to keep key employees.
- Information is a critical incentive: be honest and current with your employees.
- Try subcontractors or employee leasing services to save money.
- Hire carefully and check references.
- Taking the time to train pays off.

CHAPTER 19

RENEGOTIATING TERMS ON LOANS AND LEASES

MANAGE YOUR MONTHLY MADNESS

> *The airlines are prime examples of the need to renegotiate fixed costs of equipment leases. Fewer passengers means the need for fewer and smaller planes. Not an easy transition when airlines have been leasing increasingly larger aircraft because they were fuel-efficient. But no fully staffed plane makes money flying empty and, in the dramatic post-9/11 drop in air travel, the race was on to lower capacity and cut costs.*
>
> *The large airline lease companies themselves were run over with planes that had to be taken back by a number of small start-ups that went under. So they weren't looking to take back additional aircraft with few places to market it.*
>
> *Beginning with US Airways and its bankruptcy filing, the leasing companies had few choices. And the airlines were able to end monthly payments that were a burden in a losing environment.*

SECOND WIND

If your company has been experiencing cash flow troubles, you may have found yourself driven by debt-service needs rather than the more traditional purposes of business, such as serving your customers and making a profit. Your monthly panic is likely centered around making loan and lease payments. Too much time and energy are devoted to finding the cash to accomplish this because no alternative has been explored. I've seen goods and services under-priced and inventory liquidated below cost just to generate sufficient cash flow to meet loan or lease obligations. If you are in or close to this situation, now is the time to consider the long-term implication of this action—you are gutting your business and giving it little or no chance to move forward when the opportunity to do so arrives. There are actions you can take to ease this pressure—and you must do so immediately!

How to Renegotiate Leases

There are a vast number of types of leases. Some are straight leases and others are lease-purchase agreements. We will review the three major items you may be leasing:

1. Real property
2. Equipment
3. Vehicles

Although leases are legally binding contracts and, if enforced, can be broken only by a bankruptcy filing, they can be renegotiated and rewritten if the parties agree. You should remember going into any discussion that you have options to exercise in case of a total impasse. On the other hand, most of these options involve rejecting the balance of the lease and returning the property. If that's what you desire, a bankruptcy reorganization provides that opportunity.

In cases where you want or you need to retain the possession and use of the property in question, you will need the voluntary cooperation of the lessor-owner. In changing economic times, you may find the goal of both parties will be to keep a good working relationship, even if that means that some terms must be modified. This may be more difficult with car leases written by the major auto companies' leasing subsidiaries. They are more formal in their rules and will not readily tailor terms to meet a client's changing circumstance. At best, you may be able to get these companies to waive a few months' payments and add them to the end of the lease.

Ask Your Landlord for Help

The 10,000-square-foot building you rented when you started your business or the 50,000-square-foot warehouse you expanded into may now be far more than you need and the cost may be the burden that is sinking the boat. Perhaps you can reduce your space and rewrite your lease for fewer square feet. If you have been a valued long-term tenant, keeping you in the building may be a real incentive to your landlord. Offer a longer term for the new lease as an incentive. For example, if you have one year left and want to renegotiate terms, offer to extend the term for three to five years. The extra years may well make it worthwhile to your landlord—particularly if the space has been customized for you and may be difficult to rent to someone else.

Another way to ease the cost of your lease is to rewrite it at a lower cost in the current year with built-in increases in the future years. The overall result will be an average cost that is equal to your current rate. You will pay back the temporary decrease over the next two or three years, when you can afford it more easily. This has a cost effect on your landlord, as he will be lowering his current income, but the benefit will be in keeping some current income rather than taking the chance of losing all rent. Any willingness to accommodate you will depend on the desirability of the space. But at least you can ask.

Do You Really Need to Own Your Building?

It may have made sense to you at one time to buy the building you use instead of renting the space. The benefits included a fixed cost and perhaps room to expand. You were also building equity and, during times of inflation, that made sense. Now you may be looking for ways to contract. It may be possible to rent out unused space to another company, but that would make you into a landlord and you would be collecting rents, answering complaints, and doing maintenance for others in the building. You must consider how much of a distraction this would be from your day-to-day work.

Another solution to the issue of too much space is to sell your building. One of the benefits to you that you may not have thought of before is that, once you have paid off your mortgage, your relationship with your bank may improve. Many bankers consider their total exposure of loans to a company, including a building mortgage, when making decisions about additional loans.

If you want to stay in part of your space, it is possible to sell your building to an investor with a leaseback attached to the deal. A real estate deal that has income in place is very desirable, so a good agent should be able to market a well-priced piece of property effectively. Depending on where you are in your business life, selling off assets such as land and buildings may also be a good move in advance of someday selling the entire company.

> *There has been a recent trend in the corporate world that makes sense—selling real estate and then leasing only the needed space. Corporations such as Alcoa, PPG, and Sears that have made larger staff cuts have sold their primary but too large headquarters buildings and leased smaller space.*

At one time, I rented space for my manufacturing business from a toy distributor. I was aware that the owners turned down a substantial offer on their huge building because they claimed they couldn't find adequate space anywhere else. At the time, they were using less than half of the balance of the space; the only reason the cost wasn't destroying them was that they were deferring all of the maintenance on the structure. Only a few years later, the building and the business started fraying badly and, with little money to fix either, they both deteriorated rapidly. In the end, the business was liquidated and the real estate sold for 30% of the earlier offer. If a different decision had been made, at least the company would have had a chance to continue, even if it were a smaller operation at a different location.

> *Tip* — A business that has real estate as a part of the deal is often harder to sell than one that can be easily moved by the new owner or merged into an existing business.

Rewrite Your Equipment Leases

Some of your equipment leases may actually be lease-purchase agreements. This means that title remains in the name of the lessor until all the terms of the lease are complete and then you make one small payment at the end and the items become the property of your company. Your leases were written on the interest rate current at the time plus a premium that represents the profit to the leasing company. The terms are normally shorter than six years. Some of the leasing companies are small, locally owned operations. They go out and purchase the machine you require exactly as you may have written any specifications. Therefore, it usually isn't in their interest to repossess a piece of equipment that may be specialized for your use and more valuable to you than to anyone else.

You will still have to pay off the total value of the lease, but the term may be negotiable. And if interest rates have gone down since the inception of your lease, you may be able to increase the length of time to pay the balance at a lower rate, to lower the monthly cost.

If you have several pieces of equipment financed by individual leases, explore the possibility of combining them into one lease and, again, extending the total term to reduce the monthly cost. In the end, you will be paying out more for the total of the lease, but the value to you now is in lowering your overhead cost.

What to Do About Auto Leases

You may have leased cars for business use and now wonder if you have any options to cut the cost of these leases. While the contracts vary from company to company, there are three options to consider.

- *Turn in the unwanted cars.* Most leases will require the payment of a termination fee, which may be as low as $200. If the car is in good shape, your dealer will be the key to the other charges that may be incurred. It all hinges on the current value of the auto and the remaining payments on the lease. It's worth a trip to the dealer.
- *Trade in the cars for more economical ones.* This type of deal involves a transfer fee and other charges, depending on the condition of the vehicles and the remaining time on the lease. If you have been a frequent customer of a dealer and are likely to continue the relationship, you may receive good cooperation that will lower your costs with minimal penalty.
- *Transfer the lease to a third party.* If you can find a responsible person to take over your lease, you may be able to transfer the balance to that individual for a very small fee. The only drawback here is that your name will continue on the lease and any default will

remain your responsibility. It's a judgment call on your part.

How to Renegotiate Your Bank Debt

You may have a single loan outstanding to the bank payable over a fixed term with a regular monthly payment of principal and interest. If you have a good record of making timely payments, it may be fairly easy to arrange a restructuring of your loan, to extend the term and lower the payment of principal each month. Stop in to see your branch manager with a firm idea of what sort of new term you will require to allow you to meet the monthly cost easily. If this isn't a sufficient reduction, try a new approach: interest only for a while and then some regular principal payments and a balloon payment at the end. It might work even if you don't think that you will be able to come up with the lump-sum balloon at the end; if you have kept up with your obligation, when the balloon comes due you should be able to restructure that amount over a new term.

It gets complicated when your company has a number of loans with the same bank and the total of the debt is high. It is better to start negotiations when all payments are current and your relationship with your banker is a friendly one. Decide how much you can manage on a monthly basis and work with your banker using that number as a goal. If you combine loans and restructure the term, you may be able to substantially lower the total payment. This is not only beneficial to you and your company, but it makes life easier for your banker. Bad loans reflect on the performance of your banker, so he or she has a real interest in keeping your loans up to date. You won't know what's possible unless you try. Your banker may be your best friend in a difficult situation.

You Can Still Negotiate Delinquent Loans

If your business problems have already tarnished your relationship with your banker due to late payments, don't avoid the possibility of setting things right by working together. Perhaps you have gone out of your way to avoid your banker's calls or you no longer go into the bank office yourself, to prevent a face-to-face meeting. You won't correct the problems of your business without changing this situation, so now is the time to start.

Arrange a meeting and bring in your current financial records. Discuss your plans to turn around your operations and how long you expect to need extra consideration. If there is a way to bring your accounts current and keep them that way, your banker may be very cooperative.

If your situation has become adversarial, with some collection action already beginning, you may need to take your attorney with you or have him or her negotiate in your place. Unless your loan is well secured with liquid (cash) assets, it becomes problematic for the bank to easily enforce its collection actions. The operative word here is "easily."

Once your loans are out of the local office, they become a negative in the record of the manager, so try and catch up with any corrections and renegotiate on the local level. Most banks have workout departments, but their attitudes can vary greatly, ranging from very cooperative to very aggressive, and some have been known to be almost abusive. This is not where you want to be, if you can help it. Here you are no longer a valuable customer; now you are a delinquent borrower.

If all else fails with your secured lender, the time may have come to file for protection under the bankruptcy laws. The first effect of a Chapter 11 filing is that it stops all collection activity your bank may be effecting, even if it has begun taking a portion or all of the proceeds of your lockbox.

How to Renegotiate with Your Vendors

In an earlier section of this book, I discussed ways to conserve cash, including converting vendor credit into long-term payout. If your suppliers have been going along with this idea and you have lived up to your obligations, then you should be able to continue and perhaps even increase these types of agreements. Asking for extended terms on some purchases is also a way to increase your positive cash flow.

If you must keep the inventory needed to serve your customers over 30 days or buy small quantities of a product frequently, perhaps you can work out a consignment agreement. You will be able to buy in larger quantities and perhaps even get better prices and delivery terms, yet you will be required to pay for merchandise only when it is used. The unused material in your building will actually still be owned by your supplier. The benefit to your vendor is that this type of program locks you in as a customer; for you, the cash flow benefits are obvious.

There are many times when a vendor only reluctantly agrees to a payout of your existing bills over a period of time. Vendors may need the money for their own business or just plain resent the delay in being paid. In return for the accommodation, you might be asked to pledge an asset as security or to give a personal guarantee. I advise against this action unless it is absolutely necessary. Get good legal advice before you sign an agreement beyond your existing business relationship.

It is always possible to force new terms on landlords, lessors, and lenders, but before you take that route, try to work out your needs directly with the principals. Over the

Tip Once a loan has gone to workout, the bank has already written it off. Your future as a going concern is of little interest to that bank, so don't bother dealing with it anymore.

Banks usually have a right of offset, meaning they can pay on loan balances with checking or money market accounts kept in their hands.

long term, you will find running your operation easier if you maintain friendly working relationships.

> ## *Chapter Key Points*
>
> - Negotiating for lower interest and longer terms can ease your monthly payments.
>
> - Your rent can be lowered at least temporarily by rewriting your current lease.
>
> - Equipment lease terms can be renegotiated by extending terms or lowering interest rates.
>
> - You may be able to surrender some space back to reduce rent.
>
> - Banks do not want your assets; they want to be paid.
>
> - Your banker may be willing to work with you. Try the cooperative approach.
>
> - A bankruptcy filing can force a solution on your bank as well as other creditors.
>
> - Communicate with vendors to work out reasonable payment schedules.

CHAPTER 20

GAINING PROFITABILITY FROM CHANGE

IDENTIFY THE POSITIVES AND NEGATIVES

In every company there are areas that are more profitable than others. Companies engaged in both the sales and the service of a product may actually lose money on the service end of their operation. Or perhaps their vulnerable area is installation. You may have already identified the one phase of your operation that always seems to be a drain on resources rather than a contributor to the bottom line. However, you may be concerned that if you were to make any serious changes, you would jeopardize the entire operation.

This is something I went through in my manufacturing operation. We sold our products to distributors as well as directly to industrial end users and, needless to say, the actual users represented a larger profit margin. In addition, at times, some of our distributor customers became almost impossible to satisfy and their demands disrupted any reasonable production schedules that we tried to establish. Every time I came to the point where I was convinced that something had to be done, I agonized over it for weeks before taking action. When I finally terminated the product in question or, a few times, the customer in question, it was never easy. But, with one small exception, the result was positive. We could go back to our desired production schedule or cease inventorying an infrequently used material and our day-to-day operation became more efficient and therefore more profitable: lower overall revenue, but more on the bottom line.

Develop an Operational Strategy for Change

If you have the sense that your company has inconsistent results from some of its product lines or types of service, then you should work out a plan to correct this problem. The most effective strategy would include the following:

1. Do an operational analysis by type of business or type of customer and determine where profits or losses are derived.
2. Spend your time, money, and energy on those areas of your business that bring in the best return.
3. Consider contracting out areas of the business that show borderline or no profits.
4. You may be able to sell your "questionable" lines of business to someone who can make them profitable.
5. If you must terminate a phase of your business, do so over time and help customers to find alternative vendors.
6. Promote what your business does well.

How to Analyze Your Profit on Products or Services

Some companies have very sophisticated costing systems that provide immediate analysis by every product line or service area they perform. Large companies often break down their operations by divisions or business units and then analyze products and services by type. Small businesses usually don't have the systems or the time to accomplish this work. Yet many simple accounting programs can easily be coded to provide the data you need.

When you are making money from your overall operation, this information may not be important, but if you are struggling, the time has come to decide where the red ink is coming from and to choose the most profitable direction for your company to take.

If you are the founder of your company, you may have built it to its present level by accommodating customers in any way possible. Sometimes the demands of your customers opened up areas of business that turned out to provide high profit and high growth; other times, you did work to keep busy or because you didn't want a client to go elsewhere. Now, you must determine the impact on your bottom line of those decisions.

Look at your operation as one that makes, sells, or services a number of products or customers. Group them by some common denominator, such as all "service-only" calls in one category or all sales of one type in a category. Then allocate the direct costs of each. For example, a service call has mainly direct labor cost and a product sale will involve material as well as labor. Each will also carry an allocation of overhead. A simple analysis of a service call will look something like that shown in Figure 20-1. A simple analysis of a product sale is shown in Figure 20-2.

---

1. We charge $25/hour for service.
2. Direct labor costs $12 with 30% benefits, for a total of $15.60.
3. Overhead cost is 40% of sales revenue, in this case $10/hour.
4. On four hours of service, our costs are as follows:
   4 hours charged @ $25 = $100.00
   Labor cost of 4 hours @ $15.60 = $62.40
   Gross profit $37.60
   Overhead of $10/hour $40.00
   Loss on job ($3.40)

FIGURE 20-1. Analysis of a service call

A profit drain as small as this could be jeopardizing the overall stability of the operation and you wouldn't see it unless you looked specifically. Perhaps you think all it takes is doubling the labor costs and you will make profit. Look at each phase of your business in parts—you may be surprised.

---

1. We sell suits for $129.00.
2. Our cost of each suit is $65.00 + $4.00 freight.
3. We pay 5% commission = $6.45/suit.
4. Our overhead cost is 30% of sales = $38.70/suit.

Each sale produces the following result:

Selling price = $129.00

Less cost of goods $69.00

Gross profit $60.00

Less commission $6.45

Overhead $38.70

Profit (before tax) $14.85

FIGURE 20-2. Analysis of a product sale

As shown in Figure 20-2, $14.85 would be our profit on each sale if we were able to sell all the suits at or above their actual cost to us. If any of our inventory sells at less than cost or ends up in our back room unsold, that lowers overall profit.

Don't be shocked by what you learn from this closer look. If you find an area where you are hemorrhaging red ink, you will need to take action to correct the problem. Consider all the implications of the moves. Is the service or product actually a draw to customers and, once they are in your store, do they purchase goods and services from you that carry a healthy profit? If this is the case, then your loss may be in reality an advertising cost rather than a loss.

Grocery chains use this technique all the time. They advertise a few specials that actually lose money to attract customers into the store because virtually all of them will purchase other items. Other businesses use the same selling promotion. You can't afford any larger drain on your limited resources, so you must know the profit implications of your entire operation.

Advertise, Market, and Sell for the Profits You Need

Attracting customers by advertising low, low prices may be effective for large operations such as grocery stores, but this is likely not the draw you want to use to attract your potential customers. Remember that the message you convey will bring a specific type of client, so go after the ones you really want.

One of my clients operated a small manufacturing operation with a market to both sell and rent their finished products. Outright sales always made money, but rental was far more questionable. All their ads talked about the rental aspect of the business, because there was an eager market for the lower-cost, one-time use of the linens they fabricated. It was no wonder that more of the overall revenues came in this area, but the drain on the bottom line threatened the entire business. Our work together involved a number of operational issues, but the key one was to convert customers from renting to purchasing. Slowly we changed the emphasis in all written material from the information on rental to the value of purchase, and we even rearranged the showroom, changing displays to reflect our refocus. Rental prices were no longer posted; they were only available on request. It took six months, but slowly the desired business came and the profits rose accordingly.

SECOND WIND

The airline industry is a good example of just the opposite pattern. Airlines want the regular full-fare customers who pay a fair price for their ticket, but their message to the public doesn't say that. Most airlines ads you see are those announcing that one carrier's fares are much lower than its competitors'. Most of the fares fall below the breakeven point. The dichotomy is that while these companies really need to attract the more profitable business traveler, they are spending most of their time and attention on the low-fare, occasional flyer. It's been a long time since I have looked forward to business travel or felt that I was a valued customer, so I now make fewer trips. My attitude reflects the feelings of many other discretionary travelers, and our voluntary abandonment of the market will affect the airlines' bottom line for years to come. Attracting more people who are paying fewer dollars isn't the answer.

You don't want to appear to be completely disinterested in the other customers who are not key accounts because of their small volume or the type of product/service that they purchase. To a new business, all potential customers are important—and you never know when today's occasional buyer may turn into tomorrow's major account. Nevertheless, your outreach must stay focused on the market you want to serve.

> *You must learn to go after your best customers, not just anyone who may happen to do business with you from time to time. Advertise to them, call on them, and make them feel valued and needed, because they truly are the key to the future of your company.*

How to Profit from Using a Subcontractor

If there is a product or service that you cannot produce at a profit, that does not mean that another company isn't able to do so. A business that specializes in that specific product or service may be happy to act as your subcontractor and you both may be able to see profits from the venture.

I am particularly familiar with this situation in the sewn

products industry because of my own business experience. Our equipment and production lines could do some work effectively, but for other applications, we never quite learned the tricks to reach the required level of expertise. I was often able to purchase finished products from other manufacturers cheaper than my company could make them and then to resell them at a profit. At times, we purchased the raw material (particularly when we had a good source) and then subcontracted the labor, perhaps to an offshore operation.

Look around at your competitors as well as companies in allied industries to see if you can find new vendors that are more cost-effective. Even if the cost advantage is minimal, the value may be that you can focus your valuable time, energy, and resource where the return is higher.

> *A good example of this is using subcontractors is for installation. You may sell the product but use a subcontractor to install. They do that work all day every day and know how to do it profitably.*

Sell an Unprofitable Line to a Competitor

Before you discontinue a product or service, why not consider selling the line instead? It isn't as far-fetched as it seems. You may have machinery, inventory, a customer list, and history to sell. A competitor that wants to increase its business in this area may be more than willing to buy what you have. The key is in how you present the package.

What you are marketing has a tangible value of assets as well as the additional intangible value of the revenue and income to be considered. You should price your equipment at fair market value and salable inventory at its current value less a reasonable discount plus the premium value of the sales history (customer use and pricing) and possibly an easily identifiable name or design. If you have advertising material that includes the camera-ready art, this could be included.

Create a letter or flyer describing the business opportunity of the product or service you are trying to market and send it out to the most likely buyer. You don't want to guarantee the profits to be made in this product, but you can be optimistic about the potential that this could bring to a new owner for which this market would be a better fit and a good opportunity.

During my 20 years in manufacturing, I was both a buyer and a seller of additional product lines. As a buyer, I could buy steel cutting dies and patterns plus some raw material at half the cost and would have a ready customer base, so a revenue stream from sales would start immediately. There is a real value to that aspect. On the selling side, if my customer base for a product shrank because of plant closings or other market conditions, I could sell off a product line to another manufacturer and realize some cash for the effort. In addition, if I still had customers interested in the product, I would buy it from the other manufacturers and resell it. I did not want my customers calling the competition. In all, this is a better way to sell your excess equipment than piecemeal. It may take more time, but it is clearly worth the effort.

Liquidate Excess Inventory and Equipment

The time has come to sell off old, hard-to-sell items and put into place policies that will prevent your company from rebuilding its stock of slow movers again. This task can best be accomplished by a good software package that gives point-of-sale information that tracks how long a product has been in stock. Reorders should not be placed on items that have a very slow turn; if a valued customer wants a special order of an item, you should use all your best efforts to get the customer to accept the total quantity that you must order, so there are no leftovers to remain in your inventory for months or even years. This drain can seriously undermine a company before anyone really notices. Inventory is an asset only if it is current and salable.

When selling off old products, keep this project as separate as you can from your current business. Your inclination may be to give your regular salespeople an extra incentive to move the items, but you may end up distracting them from doing their main job, selling your profitable products. Instead of this method, why not sell your excess items to other distributors in other parts of the country? In some industries, there are services to accomplish this task, or you may even be able to ask the manufacturer to suggest possible buyers. Assign this task to one person in your organization or do it yourself. Since the urgency to find cash has passed, take your time and approach this task logically.

Retailers have another issue to consider when liquidating out-of-date merchandise. Do you want to divert the attention of your customers with racks or shelves of sales merchandise when they come into your place of business? What will be the effect on your operating profits if you drain available dollars from regular sales to breakeven transactions? If you can create other options, you should do so. How about getting together with other businesses in the area and doing a short-term sidewalk sale? The additional traffic would be of value to all of you. Perhaps you could rent a small space that has been available for a while and open an outlet shop.

> *Outlet malls were originally started to sell excess inventory outside of regular stores. They have changed over recent years. Consider a separate outlet store.*

If you have no other choice than to sell your excess in your own store, don't put it out all at once. Keep space in one section as a semipermanent clearance center and feed inventory into that area over a period of time. Eventually, you will sell most of it without distracting your regular shoppers.

Machinery can also be marketed. Use the same organized approach to sell any remaining excess equipment. Research the current value of what you have so you can price it fairly. Find all the original information on the specifications and features of the equipment and then create a flyer to send to those you have identified as potential customers. Treat this as a worthwhile sales effort and not as a junk sale. Try new businesses that may still be acquiring equipment as well as out-of-town competitors.

If your plan for the proceeds of your sale is to upgrade your current equipment, why not suggest to your equipment dealer the possibility of a trade-in? Even if the dealer doesn't do it as a normal course of business, the sale to your company may be an incentive. Most good dealers know where used machinery can be sold, so don't be afraid to ask for this additional service as part of your deal.

Intangible Assets Have Tangible Value

As you review the unused assets of your company, don't neglect items such as trademarks, contract rights, licenses, and customer information that may be of value to another company. Have you trademarked a name or patented a design that you no longer use? Do you have a contract or the option on a contract that has an economic benefit even if you are not able to take advantage of it at this time? This could be an open purchase contract for material that has gone up in price or the option to make a future purchase at a below-market price. Have you made an agreement for the likeness or logo of an individual or organization that you are unable to utilize at this time? These are some of the legal rights that may be the intangible property of your company that can be turned into cash. Have your attorney check into the transferability of any of these types of assets you may possess before you make any deals. You may be surprised at what they bring.

Another intangible asset you may have that you probably don't think about is the information you have collected about your customers. In addition to their names and addresses, your database may hold some of their buying habits. Is this information valuable to a company selling other products or services unrelated to your business? If the answer is yes, the next part of the equation is a judgment call. Could you create a marketing list and sell it to an interested company without running the risk of offending your current customers? You would charge per name for this list; if your database is large enough, this could bring a nice cash bonus.

How to Continue Serving Customers While Terminating a Product or Service

Good customer service requires advance notice. If you are unable to sell your product line to another company and are forced to discontinue offering it to customers, don't just take the action abruptly. Consider how you would feel if you had been purchasing material, a product, or a service from one company for years and suddenly it was no longer able to provide for your needs. Depending on the level of inconvenience, you may be annoyed enough to go elsewhere for your other needs as well. You don't want this to happen to your customers. It's good policy to go the extra mile for your customers.

What to Do for Your Customers

1. Notify all customers (or post the information in your place of business), at least 60 days in advance, that items or services will no longer be offered.
2. Sell off your existing inventory at a special price to allow customers to stock up.

> *Many years ago, when the Pittsburgh Steelers were at the height of their success, the rights alone to season tickets sold for over $5,000 a seat. At one time my company had the rights to 12 season tickets—a $60,000 asset that I never thought about selling, even though I could have used the cash more than the seats.*

3. Offer an alternative product or service if there is one.
4. Help customers who request the information to find out where they might be able to purchase what they need.
5. At all times, remember that your customers are a valuable asset and treat them accordingly.

How to Promote What Your Business Does Well

As years pass, it is easy to deviate from your original business concept. In fact, sometimes it's a wise move to change from the past. One of your important roles is to determine exactly which products and/or services your company is interested in selling and to be sure this is the way you position yourself through your image and promotion. You may even have to go as far as changing the name of your company to reflect what you want customers to remember about your business. You must know what you do best and make sure others know this by the image you create.

When United Airlines wanted to be thought of as a complete travel company, not simply an airline, it changed its name to Aegis, but no one liked it and the name was changed again to United Airlines. Does your name describe what your company manufactures or provides? If not, consider a change.

What does your logo or written material say about the major products or services? If you were unfamiliar with your own business, what major message would you receive from the letterhead you use or catalog you send in response to an inquiry? If it isn't completely clear to you, any potential customer is sure to be confused.

There was a time that creating a logo, brochure, or catalog was an expensive proposition. With desktop publishing capabilities, this is no longer the case. You may have someone on your staff who can use the combination of graphic software and clip art to create effective material to tell the story of your company. If you don't have in-house capabilities, there are a number of small graphics firms that can do the work cost-effectively. The franchise printing operations can reproduce your brochures, catalogs, or newsletters for pennies per item. As an example, 10 years ago, I had an agency create a brochure for my products and the cost was $6,000 with artwork and printing. I recently helped a client complete the same type of marketing material for a cost of less than $1,000. This is the positive effect of modern technology.

Your company has a story to tell: who you are, how you came into being, and what service you provide, and so forth. For many companies, this is a very interesting story and one that puts a human face on business and creates interest and loyalty among customers. Consider what your story is and make sure that your public image is consistent with those facts. In Section V, we will cover this topic further.

Chapter Key Points

- Knowing where the profits are is critical.
- Capitalizing on that knowledge is astute practice.
- Take the time to find out where your company really makes its profit.
- Contract out products or services that can be done more effectively by others.
- Sell off product lines to competitors to add to your cash cushion.
- Liquidate excess inventory or equipment.

- Don't discontinue lines without warning customers. Try to assist them in finding other sources of supply.
- Create your company image to reflect the business your company wants to attract.
- Promote yourself by accentuating the positive. Tell your story in words and actions.

CHAPTER 21

DEVELOPING CONTROLS TO KEEP THE COMPANY ON TRACK

STAY IN THE BLACK, DON'T SLIP BACK

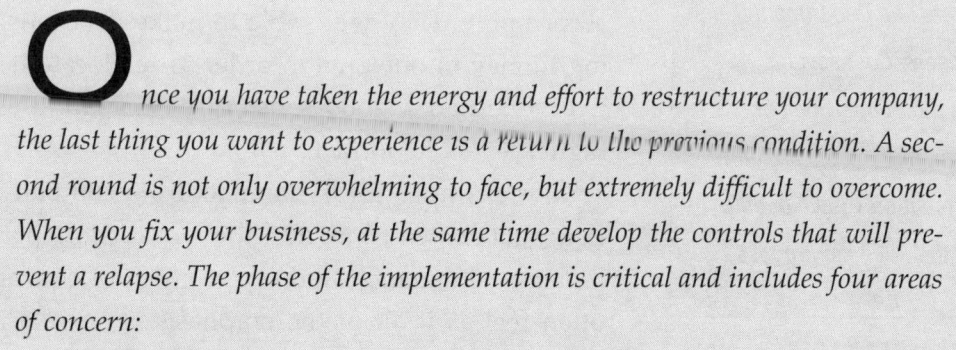

Once you have taken the energy and effort to restructure your company, the last thing you want to experience is a return to the previous condition. A second round is not only overwhelming to face, but extremely difficult to overcome. When you fix your business, at the same time develop the controls that will prevent a relapse. The phase of the implementation is critical and includes four areas of concern:

1. *Establish a budgeting procedure to use for current analysis and predicting future needs.*
2. *Create an organizational chart; learn to delegate authority.*
3. *Set accountability standards for managers.*
4. *Write and implement a job description for yourself.*

SECOND WIND

The Effective Operational Budget

Many small business owners view the process of budgeting as boring, time-consuming, and unnecessary. But the reality is that it can be a creative venture as well as a very constructive use of time. And the fact is that it is an absolute necessity to put in financial controls, particularly if you have been through difficult times and are financially fragile. You have little room for error.

In a recent managers' review with one of my clients, we discussed what had been the most productive work over the past months. I was surprised but pleased that everyone listed the budget planning as number one or two. This process gave every manager a chance to understand the financial realities of the company and plan expenses accordingly. They were able to make decisions about saving money in one area in order to reallocate it to another. Everyone had a good sense of participation as well as a higher level of contract.

For example, for a manufacturing company, the major issues of expenditure for the production personnel are repair, maintenance, and replacement of equipment. They often feel as if all of the emphasis is on sales. In budget meetings, their input would be considered and various constituencies might be able to negotiate priorities and better understand each other's needs. This process may improve productivity as well as save money, since full discussions of equipment needs and limitations are valuable to non-production managers as well.

I've worked with a number of companies that allocated virtually no money in advance to any sales and marketing expense. If an idea came along, money was spent with little thought to any organized follow-through. It was almost impossible to see if there were any results, because there

> *Any effective budget includes the input of line managers and department supervisors. Cost savings require the cooperation of everyone and people are more motivated if they have been a part of the decision process.*

was no sustainable effort. A much better solution would have been to put the budget in the hands of the sales staff and see what sort of plan they could develop.

A Budget Must Be Flexible

When you begin to create a budget, you will use certain assumptions, which will include estimates of your monthly sales, expenses that will occur based on those revenues, and expenses that are fixed overhead. There is likely to be an easy program you can use to generate a budget on your computer, but take care that you do not just insert percentages and create a document that is not well thought out. Some of your assumptions are bound to be incorrect: sales can go down because of weather, etc., and costs can go up for the same reason, due to energy costs. Be prepared to be flexible. Look at the example in Figure 21-1.

Sales	Use seasonal variances
Less cost of goods	Use target percentage (can you improve this number?—set goals)
Gross profit	Percentage
Administrative expenses	
Fixed	Such as car payments and utilities. This is a fixed number
Rent/Loans	
Interest/Leases	
Semi-variable	Here is where you have target goals such as repairs, wages, sales expenses, etc.

FIGURE 21-1. Simple budget analysis

You may project monthly or quarterly, but you should analyze only on a quarterly basis. A spike in one month may give you better or worse than expected results, so the projection isn't an accurate planning tool. Decide at the end of each quarter whether or not you need to readjust for the next period.

Creating an Organizational Chart

The question of "Who's in charge?" can be a source of confusion in many small enterprises. A number of entrepreneurs overexercise their personal control and micromanage every aspect of the operation even when there are managers in place. And they tend to use budget as a way to control: nothing is spent without their authority. If this sounds like you, now is the time to change that dynamic. You may have needed to operate this way in the early days, but if the company has grown, there aren't enough hours in the day and decisions are not being made.

The first step in delegating authority is to determine how many and which organizational areas of your operation need to be delineated. List each area and then list those in charge. Then add lines and names and those covered who will report to other than you. You will see in Figure 21-2 how this is designed. Make sure everyone is covered and not everyone reports to you.

In Figure 21-2, we looked at a small, simple manufacturing operation. Each type of business will have a slightly different configuration. In some cases, delivery drivers will report to sales. In some cases, where there is only one salesperson, the CEO may also manage that department. You want a level of organization that will allow everyone to contribute his or her best.

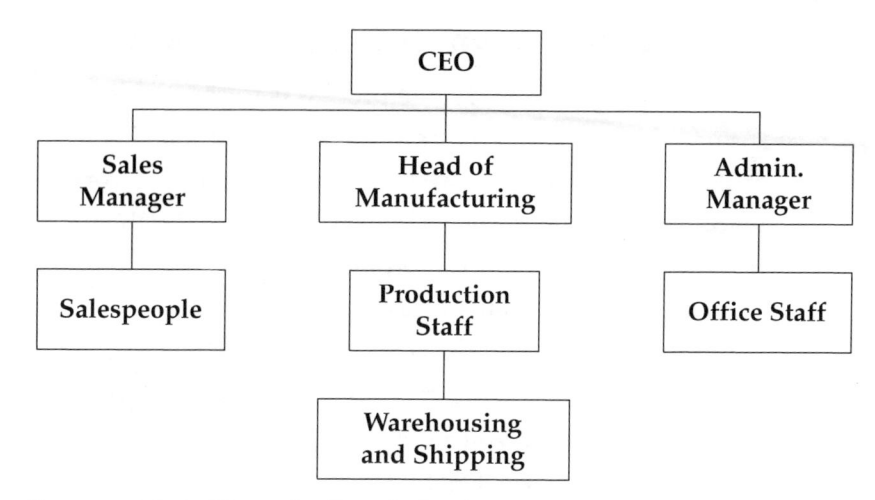

```
                    ┌─────────┐
                    │   CEO   │
                    └─────────┘
         ┌──────────────┼──────────────┐
    ┌─────────┐    ┌──────────┐    ┌─────────┐
    │  Sales  │    │ Head of  │    │ Admin.  │
    │ Manager │    │Manufact. │    │ Manager │
    └─────────┘    └──────────┘    └─────────┘
         │              │              │
    ┌─────────┐    ┌──────────┐    ┌─────────┐
    │Sales-   │    │Production│    │ Office  │
    │people   │    │  Staff   │    │  Staff  │
    └─────────┘    └──────────┘    └─────────┘
                        │
                   ┌──────────┐
                   │Warehousing│
                   │and Shipping│
                   └──────────┘
```

FIGURE 21-2. Organizational chart

Give Privileges and Expect Accountability

If you have been shouldering too much of the responsibility, this may be one of the problems that got the company into difficulty. You can't be everywhere and you can't know all of the information, so the best decisions are often made by those directly involved. Give those in authority some freedom to act and some money to allocate. Let them make choices—and remember that you haven't done everything perfectly so you shouldn't expect perfection from others. What you should expect is overall results.

Negotiate with those in each area how their performance will be measured. It may be a sales goal, a cost control goal, or a productivity goal. Make it reasonable, be sure both of you are in agreement, and then expect the outcome to match. If it exceeds, consider a reward. If it doesn't, consider a change. It is time to be specific about what must happen for the company to survive and thrive. Your job is to choose the right managers, monitor their progress, and take action when it is needed.

Create Your Own Job Description

The final phase of the change process is to change yourself. Companies slip into crisis more readily if no one is paying attention and things slip through the cracks. Everyone wants to share in the success; now it is time to let them take responsibility for all of the problems as well.

The time has come to ask yourself critical questions about what your job at the company really should be at this time. Are you spending too much time second-guessing everyone else? Are you paying too much attention to old customers who have become friends and not developing new ones? Could the existing clients be served by staff? Are you researching new industry trends? Have you become too busy with outside activities, whether for fun or for the community, that you are not spending enough of your time on the business? Have you become a caretaker of your company while the business environment around you continues to change?

By now you know the truth: it is not as easy as most people think to work for yourself and report to no one. This requires a substantial amount of self-discipline and a high degree of organization. The time to begin to change is now!

List the major functions in the company that *must* be done by *you*. Be sure that you do not include tasks that are better accomplished by someone else in the organization. Now take this process one step further and consider what functions (such as marketing or financial analysis) are not assumed by anyone else and decide if you should handle these areas— even if they are ones you don't like.

Write a job description for yourself as if you were hiring a replacement. Determine your daily, weekly, and monthly tasks and create a calendar for them. Then go about doing your job as you would want others to go about

> *The role of CEO should be focused on leadership, planning, and troubleshooting. You steer the ship, so it's important to keep checking the horizon.*

completing theirs. What the company needs is long-term stability; it begins with you.

Chapter Key Points

- Chaos is an open invitation to the forces that can destroy any business regardless of its previous success. An important step in recovery is creating controls for the future.

- Budgets are an excellent planning device. Create one with the input of managers and use it for review to monitor progress.

- Delegate authority. Create and use an organizational chart. Allow for freedom and expect accountability.

- Create your own job description. You may find some new areas to master and lead.

SECTION V

▲ ▲ ▲

ENSURING THE FUTURE

CHAPTER 22

ESTABLISHING BENCHMARKS

PLAN FOR PROSPERITY

> Turnaround work can go on for months, as you first stabilize your business and then make the changes that will put it on the right track. No one who has ever been through this will minimize the effort involved and it would not be surprising that you have less energy and enthusiasm for both the work and the company at this point. In the next few chapters, we are going to discuss a number of different alternatives that will allow you to share the work or perhaps to exit altogether. But first you must establish some benchmarks along the way that will keep you on the path to prosperity.

What Growth Do You Expect?

Most, but not all, companies experience serious revenue loss at the beginning and even during a turnaround period. It may be caused by general economic conditions or it may be simply that the company does not have the resources to serve all of its existing customers. You must plan for new growth from external sources.

Any understanding of the cash flow requirements of growth will show you that you will need new working capital in order to fund the business. The higher the new sales revenue, the greater the need for cash to pay for materials and wages. Depending on the type of business, cash receipts could lag sales by 60 or 90 days. Your vendors are unlikely to give you sufficient credit and you will find yourself back in a cash flow quagmire again.

So, too much growth may be as much of a problem as too little. The only answer is to plan for it by setting goals that are reasonable, such as 5%-10%, and then preparing to fund the growth with vendor credit or easier financing tools, such as contract loans. These are funds borrowed directly against confirmed written business orders and paid back directly from customer proceeds. You may be able to access this type of loan even if your credit has been damaged by recent events.

Where Will the Growth Come From?

Real and sustainable profitability comes from securing additional business in the areas where your margins are secure. Business for the sake of cash flow can be dangerous. For example, the airlines make most of their profit from the business travelers, who usually buy the higher-price tickets. But in order to fill more of the seats, they offer lower-priced tickets as well. When business travel is soft, deep discounting sometimes takes place and the result is the average revenue per mile goes down drastically. In the post-9/11 era, that was the only way to fill planes and the industry suffered record-breaking losses.

Guard against doing business for the sake of cash flow, particularly when you are fragile coming off a period of difficulty. You must not mistake cash flow for profitability—growth at a loss or breakeven can undermine all of your hard work. Anyone can give products and services away. You want to sell them at a profit and that requires focusing on where you can find customers/clients who find value in what you do and how you do it. Know where this market is and pursue it.

> *Real and sustainable profitability comes from securing additional business in the areas where your margins are secure. Business for the sake of cash flow can be dangerous.*

What Profitability Levels Are Your Goal?

You must set and monitor goals for both gross profit margins and net profits. The first is directly related to the second. If, during any period, you are not meeting these goals, give immediate attention to finding out why and correcting the problem. A drop—even if it is small and seems temporary—should be viewed as a warning and investigated.

What New Technology Is Expected?

Few businesses haven't seen major improvements in productivity as a result of new technology. In fact, in most industries, it is almost impossible to compete without the newer generation of equipment. Labor-intensive businesses no longer need as many employee hours to complete the same jobs and even administrative personnel have been replaced by easy-to-operate software packages that allow one employee to do the work formerly performed by two or more. You must know what is available and be prepared to phase it in to your operation.

> **Tip** The rush into e-commerce was costly for many companies. Don't rush into the latest fad until there is some idea where it is going. Leave that for companies with more money.

Preparation begins on two fronts—finding the financial resources to lease or purchase what you need and training the human resources already in place to maximize the potential. Set goals and timeframes to get on board or the technology train will leave the station without you.

Study What the Future Holds

Nothing remains static: products change, demands change, and how needs are met changes. What you did last year may be outdated in a few years.

Sometimes it's gradual and sometimes it's instant, but change in business is a constant. Do you know where your industry is going? Do you know what signs you will be looking for? And most important, do you know what you will do to meet the changes? If you aren't sure, you need to be thinking about it now. This is a very important aspect of your job—strategic planning for the future.

Can You Prepare Your Finances?

Stabilizing the cash position of your company is an indication of a successful turnaround. If you are able to renegotiate the cash demands of loans and leases that allow you to return profitability and remain profitable, that is a successful turnaround. But a secure future requires that you take this one step further.

Every company needs a reserve of working capital to maintain payments and pay expenses such as payroll while waiting for cash to come in. You may want to become an opportunistic investor at some point. That means being in position to take advantage of special deals for inventory or raw material, which takes money.

Rebuilding your financial base will take time, but you need to set goals to accomplish this. Surely you don't ever

SECOND WIND

Rough Journey for Travel Industry

The travel industry has undergone dynamic change over the past few years. The Internet brought a vast number of new players into the field, using software instead of people has saved money, and the 24/7 nature of the Web has increased convenience. Agencies that want to survive, much less prosper, have to redefine the value of their service and add on-line access as well.

Airlines and hotels projected unlimited growth in their future, adding planes, routes, and rooms while ignoring a rapidly maturing economy and the growing acceptance of teleconferences. Then a sudden event struck fear into some travelers and years of profits melted into massive losses. Part of this change was predictable.

want to return to the situation you just corrected. Putting money aside, just in case, is the best form of protection.

Are There Ways to Leverage Growth?

The final step to establishing future stability is to fully explore the possibilities of joining forces with other individuals or organizations in partnerships and alliances. You may have been motivated by the challenge to "go it alone" and you certainly have proven that you can do just that. Perhaps now is the right time to expand your horizons beyond that initial goal.

One of my clients who had a mid-sized printing company actually ended a turnaround on a far better note than anyone expected. Late in the game, he joined forces with a pre-press service group and they combined some of the resources of both companies to integrate the two operations, although they remained separate businesses.

This gave the printing company extra services to market and access to new customers. The service group also had access to new customers and additional equipment to use. New directions may be opened this way.

Chapter Key Points

- You should set new goals and benchmarks as you secure the future of the company.
- Plan for growth in the areas that are most profitable.
- Know your best customers and serve their needs.
- Keep up with technology and use your resources to include it to improve productivity.
- Understand the direction of the market and use this information as a planning tool.
- Plan for future capital needs and save the money you will need.
- Consider where you can form new business relationships to leverage the growth of your company.

CHAPTER 23

FORM NEW PARTNERSHIPS AND STRATEGIC ALLIANCES

HOW TO WORK WELL WITH OTHERS

T&V Printing was a high-end offset printing company whose work was known and respected. Most of their customers used designers to create the catalog and mail pieces that T&V produced. So their selling expense wasn't high, but their customer base was limited.

When business slowed up, it was difficult to pay the overtime for the beautiful building they had fixed up when they expanded to a larger press. And they never filled the building completely.

In passing, one of their designers mentioned that she would love to cut her costs by getting out of the big office she occupied.

The idea struck the printer and her designer simultaneously. Here was a chance to share space, costs, and ideas and try to grow together. In addition to paying rent, the designer also created marketing material for the printer. It turned out to be a great alliance.

Both businesses grew with lower overhead and greater access to resources.

In the early days, when you started your business, you may have been drawn to the independence of being an entrepreneur. There is an attraction of "being your own boss" and you don't see the downside of that until you are in the midst of a business crisis. Struggling with problems, you may have begun to realize the isolation of being on your own and there are likely times when you would have welcomed having a partner. Now may be the time to explore options that will bring new energy, ideas, and advice into the company. Project partnerships and joint ventures may be for short-term events or for the long haul, but these strategic alliances may be just what your company needs at this time.

What Is a Strategic Alliance?

This term covers a variety of business activities from co-op advertising to becoming partners on a project. Any time you join forces with another company or individual for your "mutual benefit," you have formed a strategic alliance. You are not working for them and they are not working for you—you are both working simultaneously for yourselves and each other.

Some Reasons to Form Strategic Alliances

There are a vast variety of business goals that companies can meet more quickly and cost-effectively by joining forces. The following are some examples of what you can accomplish through alliances.

Joint Sales and Marketing

You see the result of this type of alliance on a day-to-day basis, but you may not identify it as such. Food manufacturers advertise with grocery stores, beer companies run promotions with restaurants, and publishers run promotions with bookstores. Ask one of your large suppliers if they do shared advertising and promotions—you may be surprised to find out that there is already a budget established to handle just such a request. They may have a limited program or they may be willing to listen to your ideas.

How about cosponsoring an event with another company in order to stimulate demand for both of you? Or a multiple-company event like a sidewalk sale or the joint promotions sponsored by the owners of shopping malls? Ask around: if there's nothing for you to join, you could think up your own opportunities. You pay a part of the advertising, but get full value from the increased traffic.

> *Many charity golf tournaments are sponsored by more than one company. Each gets the benefit of getting its name in front of a very selective audience.*

Handle Larger Contracts

A contractor called me to help him put together the documents for a fairly large loan. He had a small company that often was either too busy or too quiet—he found it almost impossible to secure the right amount of work. This is typical of the type of business.

Looking over the budget he had put together for this new financing, one thing was evident. While the project he had accepted was profitable, once it was over it would be more than just a strain to make the payments on the loan for new equipment, etc. I asked tough questions about what project would be next and he really didn't know. He knew only that this was an opportunity he couldn't turn down.

Instead of going forward as he had originally planned, we determined that the best solution would be to join forces with another small contractor and they could jointly handle the job. This wasn't the case of hiring a subcontractor—they formed a joint venture, sharing both the risk and the profits. If the job came in under budget, which it did, they both made extra money. It worked out well enough that eventually the two companies merged.

Not all new contracts are wonderful opportunities. Some may strain the resources of your company enough to put it at risk. To minimize the risk, why not consider a strategic alliance with another company in a similar business? Between the two of you, combining work forces and resources, a large contract may be far more beneficial.

Of course, trust is a factor here; that begins with your choice of partners. Make sure you know the company and it has a good track record. The new guy on the block who has big intentions may not be what he seems. We will discuss the details of negotiations between alliance partners later in this chapter.

Tip — Productivity is about full utilization, so what better way is there to maximize value than to share with another company what you do not need on a full-time basis?

Shared Resources

For the printing company I used as an early example, both they and the service bureau were able to use some of the same equipment, particularly a proofing system. Their challenge was to determine the percentage of usage for each and share the expense fairly as well.

It may be equipment, it may be space, and it may even be personnel, but you may be able to utilize additional resources belonging to someone else on an as-needed basis.

Joint Product Development

Did you know that many larger corporations that produce raw materials are prepared to help companies develop new or greater uses for their products and even subsidize such projects? Whether you manufacture or even resell products, if you have come up with an innovation, go directly to the source of your materials and ask what programs may be available.

You may be surprised to consider the government, particularly the federal government, as a potential partner for an alliance. If you can develop something that may be of use to any federal agency, you may be able not only to get it funded but also to access technical information developed by the agency you are working with. There is a central clearing agency called the National Technology Transfer Center (www.nttc.edu) that maintains a comprehensive database of completed and ongoing research in a number of areas. Perhaps you can make Uncle Sam your R&D partner. And then, the government can become a major customer as well.

Virtual Corporations

You can form a business that exists only for a single purpose and then dissolves when the work is over. That's one of the definitions of a virtual corporation.

A number of years ago, Mick Jagger went on an extensive world tour, a venture that even business magazines described as a virtual corporation. For six months, companies owning all sorts of sound, construction, and transportation equipment joined forces with some service groups that feed and move people. Together they worked as one business. Their product was the concert and they produced it all over the world.

This business did not exist before the tour began and disbanded after it was over, but for that one project the partner companies operated seamlessly as one company. Can you find such a project?

What to Look For in a Strategic Partner

Before you go out and make any arrangements with another company, take the time to analyze your needs.

- What exactly do you hope to accomplish? What resources will you require?
- Are you looking for equipment? How much use time will you need?
- Are you looking for workers and what level of expertise do you require? (If you have to train workers from another company, perhaps you ought to hire and train your own.)
- Do you need financial resources? How much of the cost or credit can you contribute?
- Are you looking for a long-term relationship or is this one project all you anticipate?
- Are you looking for expertise in an area other than your own?

Once you have determined what you need, then you must find the organization and the individual who will bring these skills and resources. In many instances, this will not be as easy as it seems.

Your new partner will have access to much of the information that until now was very private. Your partner will get to know who your customer is—perhaps learn some trade secrets about how you produce or sell your products and/or services and have insights on your costs as well as your pricing strategy. Take care in making your selection.

Consult with an Attorney

Before doing anything that puts your business at risk, you need to see a good business attorney. The best protection you will have is by selecting honorable partners, but you will find further protection by putting all of your agreements in writing. This protects you in several ways. First, if there hasn't been a meeting of the minds in terms of expectations and responsibilities, you are more likely to find out once you have put this on paper. Second, the thought that an agreement can be enforced will keep everyone on their toes. Finally, if a partner violates the terms of the agreement, legal action is possible. The fact is, however, that it often costs as much to sue as you might collect.

Remember when you are working on the agreements that it is foolish to spend big money on legal fees over a piece of work that is not very big. One way to keep the costs down is for you and your partner to write your joint understanding and then take it to the attorney to review. Having an attorney draft the document will cost more and usually produce a document that is far more complex than you need.

Begin with a Confidentiality Agreement

Even before you have completely negotiated the terms of your project contract, you will be sharing some private information. Before you do that, the two of you need to sign an agreement that neither one will disclose or use any of the shared information and any violation may result in a cause of action. The elements of this agreement are as follows:

1. The type of negotiations anticipated (joint venture, merger, sale)
2. The full scope of the information to be shared
3. The joint agreement of both partners not to use any private information shared for purposes other than that identified by this agreement
4. The length of time the agreement is in effect

The Project Documents

After you have successfully negotiated the elements of your project, one of you needs to put it in form of a business plan. This doesn't have to be as comprehensive as one you would use when starting a company, but it should cover all of the elements of shared resources, responsibilities, and rewards. The areas to be covered are as follows:

- The Scope of the Project: What is the full range of activities the two companies will be jointly accomplishing?
- The Shared Resources: Who will contribute what in terms of workers and equipment?
- The Financial Arrangement: How will joint expenses be handled? How will individual obligations be retired? Remember: one partner may, in some circumstances, be responsible for the unpaid bills of the other—or they may be passed on to the customer and deducted from the payment.
- Benchmarks for Completion: Both of you have responsibilities and both must meet dates. If one is unable, what happens? The whole project will suffer and reflect on both of you.

> Once you have created such a document and your lawyer has assured you that it conforms to standards, you can use it for other negotiations as well. Just fill in the appropriate information.

Creating an Operating Agreement

Take all the items covered in the plan and convert them into an operating agreement. The two entities jointly agree to accomplish the task using specified resources with agreements as to financial responsibilities and rewards identified in the specific time frames. The document will need to be as simple or as complex as the project. Again, show this to your attorney for review, to make sure it conforms with legal requirements.

A Word About Contracts

It is always best to have your business dealings committed to writing, but do not expect that it will ever be easy to enforce any violations. Lawsuits take time and seldom benefit anyone but the lawyers. Try instead to make an arrangement that will work.

Chapter Key Points

- Synergy is the extra push you get from the combined efforts of two entities. Try this for your business as well.

- Joint marketing efforts can save money and increase sales.

- Before you buy new equipment, find out if there is some available that is currently underutilized.

- A strategic alliance is a two-way street. You both have risks and responsibilities in addition to possible rewards.

- A joint venture is a good way to try out a new undertaking. You will always learn from the experience.

- Put everything in writing, but understand the limitations of legal remedies.

Tip The most important phase of writing the contract may be the face-to-face negotiations that begin the process.

CHAPTER 24

PLAN FOR SUCCESSION

PASSING THE TORCH

> Lou's father had been president of their industrial supply company for over 31 years. He had taken the small company his father began and grown it to a multi-million dollar business. For years, it prospered.
>
> In the early 1990s, many of their customers downsized their manufacturing operations and needed far fewer supplies. Lou and his dad grew increasingly concerned and Lou wanted to take some drastic action. Dad was less motivated; he had been through cycles before and business always came back. Lou disagreed; he felt changes were permanent and they had better begin aggressive moves themselves.
>
> For the first time, father and son began to argue, although Dad would admit that there were times he thought Lou was right. The moment had come to pass on the torch. Father and son went to an accountant and lawyer, set a value for the company, and made a buyout agreement. The price was a bit high, but the payout time was reasonable. Within three years, Lou had created a much different, somewhat smaller, and fairly profitable organization. Dad was getting his money and Lou had gotten the freedom to make his own decisions.

A substantial number of closely held companies have multiple generations of the same family involved in the business operation. Current management may very well be the second generation already, as it is often a mature company that finds itself slipping into difficult times. Perhaps the business did not change sufficiently with the times and that is why profitability diminished and a turnaround was needed. It may also be the case that current management has been losing interest and not operating as efficiently as the business requires.

Now, everyone has been under the pressure of recent workloads and the need for a succession strategy is greater than ever. Can it be done successfully at this point?

You must realize that it is very difficult to pass on a fragile company without a genuine understanding of what it *can* and *cannot* do going forward. It cannot provide ongoing income for a nonworking family member who has chosen to retire: payment without productive contribution is the quickest way to get back into real trouble. So if the financial resource is critical to the current owner(s), an outright sale or liquidation of assets may be required. We will discuss this strategy in depth in the next chapter.

But, if the current owner(s) can retire on other assets or wait for some time, if ever, to be compensated for the equity, succession is still possible. It is the dream of many business owners to pass on the company, but the statistics prove how tricky this is. According to recent statistics compiled by the SBA, only about 35% of all closely held companies pass on to the second generation and about 16% make it to the third. Not the best odds.

> *According to recent statistics compiled by the SBA, about 35% of second-generation owners succeed and only 16% go successfully into the third generation. A thought to consider.*

Succession Must Be Based on Ability

Any business requires strong and talented leadership in

order to make it successful, but one that is emerging from a tough period has an even greater need. And the ability must also be accompanied by real desire. You have learned that this isn't just a job, but a way of life. Does your successor understand the concept as well?

If this was your vision and you created the venture based on that, have you been able to inspire your successor enough to carry on in the same way or better? Now is the time, if you haven't done this before, to have a real heart-to-heart conversation about the company and its future. The reality is that a certain number of offspring are in the family business not because they want to be, but because they are trying to please their parent(s). This is not the desired successor for any company, particularly a fragile one.

In my consulting practice, I have seen this repeatedly and one of the reasons is the inability of the offspring to tell their parent how they really feel. This may be an excellent place for an outside consultant to help. And there are specialized family business consultants who are well equipped to facilitate these discussions. Many universities sponsor family business centers, which may be a valuable resource in helping you find such a specialist, who will schedule family meetings and encourage an open and honest dialogue.

Most small business owners do not realize that a company needs to be groomed for a sale. It may take as long as three years to correct problems on the balance sheet and the income statement to make the operation attractive to a new owner. By the same token, it may take some time to get a company in shape to turn it over to a new family owner. Remember: there is a learning curve for any new executive, including the offspring of the founder, so the early days of a new administration may not be quite as productive and profitable as the old one. The company should be in sturdy shape before the transition is made.

Succession Requires Managerial Talent

Along with rebuilding the venture, you must prepare your successor. Once you have determined that the torch will be passed, the time has come to turn over some of the real decision making to the heir apparent. Perhaps it begins with control of a project or a product line, but it needs to start. Your successor needs to learn some new skills in terms of exercising the right amount of control and those around him or her need to become comfortable with a new authority.

I know this problem personally, because I took over a family business very suddenly after my father died. Employees weren't sure how I could continue and some left. Vendors were more cautious with credit. Even some customers thought that they had better consider alternative suppliers. The banker became so impossible to deal with that we had to find a new one. Having experienced the problems, I know how they affected my early days.

So the first step in a successful family succession is to determine when it will take place and then begin to delegate more authority to the one who will take over the reins. Not any easy task for many entrepreneurs, but one that is clearly necessary. The next step is to make the deal between the two of you and put it in writing.

> *Having the change take place gradually allows employees, vendors, customers, and bankers to get to know the new CEO in a comfortable way. A sudden change in leadership disadvantages everyone.*

The Succession Agreement

I have heard a father say to his son, "I'm retiring to play golf, you just send me a check every month." Not only is this an unrealistic way to turn over a business, but it can only lead to trouble.

There are many reasons that a succession must be dealt with the same as the sale of the company. Primary among them are the tax implications. The seller must establish the value for purpose of reporting gains or establishing the inheritance tax. The buyer also needs to have a definite selling price for tax planning.

Ownership title must pass in a clear way so that everyone understands who owns the company. If this has been a major source of family perks, that may be over and this change is more easily accepted if it accompanies an ownership change. Dad or Mom must also understand that he or she no longer has the keys to the piggy bank.

And speaking of the bank, it will require that anyone having over 20% ownership of the business sign personally on any loans. A change of ownership that is done formally should also include a release of any loan on credit liability from the previous owner.

Any debt or long-term payout due to the former owner must be recorded on the balance sheet as an ongoing expense for the company. For the previous owner, this line item will establish the payments as cash for the sale of assets rather than having them be treated as ordinary income, which could affect Social Security income and tax payments. So sit down with the company attorney and draw up a formal sales agreement. It will make life easier for both of you.

List what is to be sold. (It may not be every asset: perhaps a building or a large piece of equipment will be retained by the current owner and leased back to the company.) Do all of the receivables go or will some be collected and retained by the seller? This may be a way to get cash into the hands of the selling party. What is the full purchase price and what are the terms of payment? In the case of any failure to pay, are there any terms of remedy?

Another reason to keep a clear paper trail is in case the successor cannot or does not wish to continue with the purchase and ceases making payments. If the remaining

> *Many banks will not allow payout to former owners while there are loans due. The payout may be subordinate debt (secondary), so the banks get their money first.*

amount of the debt is going to be written off as a loss for tax purposes, a completely documented paper trail will be required.

The transition between generations is never easy. While both parties may be from the same family, they may have far different views and styles and the owner may not approve of all of the decisions of the successor. One way to minimize the tension between the two is to treat this transaction formally, officially, and in writing.

Succession to a Unrelated Party

You don't have to have an interested daughter or son in order to find someone to succeed you in your business. Perhaps you have one or more long-time employees with the ability and desire to carry on with the company. There are a number of ways to handle the process of transferring ownership.

You may establish a *buy-sell* agreement at any time that establishes at least a first refusal right to purchase the company. It may be at a price established at the signing or at a formula put into place at that time. This agreement may also be funded in a variety of ways, including the ownership of a life insurance policy.

Perhaps an outright buyout would stretch the resources of your candidate. Perhaps a gradual acquisition of the ownership would be more feasible. The challenge will be in establishing value that may change over a period of time as the assets grow or profitability increases. For a period of time, you will have some minority shareholders and they will feel greater responsibility for the company.

When you are ready to retire, the shares that buy you out will be sold for a lump sum or payments, if you can handle this arrangement. You do not want to retain a

> *At the end of an arduous period of turnaround, new blood may be the best thing for the company. If you have someone with the drive and the desire, why not give that person a chance?*

minority interest in the company, but you do want a security interest in the assets until you are fully paid out. In case of a failure to pay, you may once again be the owner of the company.

Chapter Key Points

- Family business succession is not as easy as it seems. There are some important issues to consider.
- The potential new owner must have the ability to do the job, not just the right parent(s).
- A fragile company cannot be passed on successfully. It must be strengthened first.
- Provide training and support for your offspring before turning over the reins.
- Put your deal in writing! Make the agreement financially and legally sound.
- Succession may also be planned with nonfamily employees. Minority ownership may present problems, so be careful from the beginning.

CHAPTER 25

ADDITIONAL EXIT STRATEGIES—MERGERS AND SALES

FINDING A WAY OUT

> Linda had been in the restaurant business for years, running one and then two highly successful eateries. Well-known and well-respected people, including bankers and food suppliers, assumed that the second place would be no problem. But it was. She was such a detail-oriented person that two locations that couldn't be watched all the time made her far less efficient and she couldn't serve customers as well and she let the record keeping slide as well.
>
> After having one very profitable place and the successful launch of the other, it was quite a shock to realize that the two were dragging each other down. Painful as it was, selling one location was the only solution.
>
> Much interest was focused on the original site and Linda was reluctant. But, given its steady income over the years, buyers felt confident about continuing to make profit.
>
> A deal was soon made and Linda found out, with the additional cash and free time, it was more satisfying for her to focus on the new spot and create another institution.

There are a number of reasons to plan a complete exit strategy, one that usually involves selling out to an unrelated individual or company. It may be that you are at a retirement age and had wanted to do this before the company began experiencing difficulties. It may be that the problems have tainted your relationships in the industry and continuing will create too much of a burden for you and the company. It also may be that there is no way for you to provide the future capital needs of the company, so a new entity is an absolute necessity.

Be honest about exactly where the company is at this moment and where you are in relationship to that position. Then make a decision about what exit strategy to follow. Remember: everyone stops working at some time—you just have more work to do before you can stop. A golden parachute and a gold watch aren't in the cards for an entrepreneur.

Consider the Possibility of a Merger

You may not have to sell the company outright; you may be able to merge with another company to increase markets, efficiency, and profitability. The additional resources may be the key to long-term prosperity. There are several versions of company mergers.

Entities Remain Independent

In this case, a holding company decides to build a network of businesses in a similar industry to take advantage of purchasing and sales opportunities. One by one, it purchases smaller organizations so that a number of companies, each retaining a separate name and some operational independence, all have the same parent company. The markets may or may not know of the corporate association.

There are a vast number of examples of this type of

business operation, from those you might recognize—such as Federated Department Stores, which operate Macy's and Bloomingdale's and Burdines along with a number of other well-known store brands—to industrial companies you would not recognize—such as Archer Daniels Midland.

Merge/Sale

While two companies that are perhaps of equal size merge their assets, only one becomes the surviving entity. Former owners may retain almost equal financial interest, but only the surviving identity goes forward. Most duplicated services are consolidated into one location, so job loss is likely.

Consolidation: An Entire New Company Emerges

The operating companies merge to form an entirely new business. Each unit may still perform the same work as before in terms of products or services, but the overall activities such as financial, administrative, and sales will be conducted by the new company that is formed.

The Benefits of a Merger

There are a number of improvements you could make to your business by merging with another company. The following are the primary areas to consider.

Geographical Expansion

You may have been selling your product in one region and have much of the business in your area. One way to expand is to merge with one or more similar companies in other parts of the country.

Combined Purchasing Power

There is always pricing pressure to contend with. While you may be able to reduce overhead to lower costs, the price of your goods or material may be inflexible at your current purchasing volume. A merger that increases the total amount of purchases will allow more leverage to negotiate terms. Lower costs means you can be more competitive and likely more profitable.

Combined Services

You have to maintain complete overhead functions to support your current level of business. You may have 10 people who are doing the advertising, marketing, billing, payroll and collections, etc. A merger with a compatible company will give you the combined volume at likely only a fraction of the total overhead, as one location can do the functions for all the companies—another bottom-line benefit.

> *For example, in the fast food industry you have KFC and Taco Bell, which often sell both lines from the same store.*

Access to New Technology or Products

A competitor in another location may have developed or purchased new technology that produces better-quality products or does the work more efficiently. For example, perhaps it is using e-commerce tools that allow for on-line purchasing. You may not have the $100,000 needed to develop and manage a site. A merger between the two companies would allow shared use of the technology—a great way to grow profitably.

The same scenario holds true with regard to new, improved products. Combining two or more companies in a merger allows them to cross-sell a wider variety of products.

Diversification

If you have a good bit of the market for your product or

service and there seems to be no way to grow, a merger with a business providing different products or services to the same customer may be the way to go. A merger offers both companies diversification without the cost of setting up a new business. This can smooth out the cyclical bumps.

Finding a Merger Partner

There are many companies that might make a complementary partner for your business—those already in the industry or in allied businesses are the most logical. One of your problems may be that you are reluctant to make contact with others to express your interest in such an arrangement. You may not want to let it become public that you are considering such a move. Why not use a consultant or your accountant or attorney to make a blind inquiry? Letters can be sent asking if there is any interest and initial contacts can be made without your intention becoming public knowledge.

You may also go to a business broker to find such a deal, but remember: there will be a cost and a broker may shop you around more than you would really welcome.

Getting Ready for a Sale or a Merger

Whether you are merging your company or preparing for an outright sale, there are steps you will have to take to ensure that the deal you are making is the best one possible for you and for your company. You cannot rush the process, as it is complicated and can get off track fairly quickly. Along the way you must think through what you are doing. Then, once you are negotiating with a buyer, you must understand their game plan as well.

Here are seven steps you are likely to take along the way to a successful sale.

SECOND WIND

> *Pricing a small business for sale is more of an art than a science. Among other things, it may depend on general economic conditions, such as interest rates, and on the buyer.*

1. Know What You Are Selling

There are several ways a business is valued. You should understand the basics so that you can set a reasonable price for your business and evaluate any offers that you may receive. A going concern is valued either for its earnings or based on its assets. You may even create a hybrid of the two methods. Each business has special elements to consider; you need to know yours well before you begin the process.

Most service businesses without high levels of tangible assets are valued based on a multiple of their earnings before interest, taxes, depreciation, and amortization (EBITDA). Depending on the industry, you may receive from a low of three times earnings to a high of 10 times.

A capital-intensive business will receive value for the assets it is selling. Do not just rely on the book value of the assets, as depreciation may have written off property and equipment that has value far greater than listed. This may be particularly true if you have unused or underused capacity that a buyer could maximize.

If you are selling to an individual, that person may be more conservative in the price he or she is willing to pay because the growth of the company is based on the existing level of business. However, if you are selling to another business, it may be able to leverage your customers and equipment to a much higher level much more quickly. Consider that when deciding what a fair market price might be.

2. Clean Up Any Mess

If you were putting your house up for sale, you would make sure that it was clean and fixed up to appeal to any potential buyer. You need to do the same with any business you intend to sell.

A cleanup of the business premises is a good idea. Make sure the office looks organized and under control. It will give the buyer greater confidence in the accuracy of your records. The physical facilities of the company—showroom, factory floor, or warehouse—ought to look busy but under control. Look at equipment to make sure it doesn't have dirt and rust on it. Perhaps a bit of painting will make surfaces seem fresher and everything more efficient.

Sell off inventory that is just taking up space and unneeded equipment as well. That makes the space look neater and also puts some cash in your pocket.

But it is more important to scrutinize for problem areas in your balance sheet and income statement. You need to put the best foot forward from a financial standpoint—it will pay off in many ways. First, a good trend will attract buyers and give them confidence about making the purchase. Second, a higher level of earnings will bring you a higher offer and you will end up with more cash for the sale.

Begin by paying down debt. Liquidate inventory and excess equipment and use the money to pay off vendor credit and bank loans. Make sure that the company has a positive net worth.

Look at your income statement and make sure your margins are as good as you can get them. If you are paying some personal expense along with general administrative debt, slow it down if you can't stop it altogether. If any nonworking family members are on the payroll, now is the time to take them off. Show your potential buyer how profitable your company can really be.

3. What About a Business Broker?

Do you want to handle this sale yourself or is it something you feel absolutely ill-equipped to do? There are some good reasons to turn the process over to a business broker.

- A broker may help you evaluate the company and set a price.

- A broker can attract potential buyers who would otherwise not know of your company.
- A broker should prequalify all potential buyers to make sure you only spend time with serious inquiries.
- A broker will handle much of the paperwork.

Remember, though, that the cost for these services is substantial, perhaps 15% of the selling price. If you already have potential candidates, perhaps you and your attorney can handle the negotiation and save the fee.

4. Sign Confidentiality Agreements

Before you begin to turn over any sensitive information, always have a potential buyer sign an agreement about nondisclosure. Remember: these are hard to enforce, because you would have to prove that the information was, in fact, used and what damage that use caused your company. So, do it—even if it may not help.

The best thing to do in these situations is to be careful and trust your instincts. Make sure your potential buyer is a serious buyer and go with the sense of trust (or distrust) you develop.

5. Make the Deal

It is often best to allow others to handle the negotiations. You are too close to the situation and any criticism from the other party may make you defensive. So, while you may do the "dog and pony show," let an advisor hammer out the specific terms.

First, you will have to sell the allure and possibilities of the company. That's your department. Meet with prospective buyers, show them through, and perhaps prepare a package of marketing material. Tell the story in an honest but optimistic way.

The next step is to determine what they want to buy—it isn't all that simple. A business can be sold in several different ways—the purchase of assets or the purchase of the stock assuming all assets and liabilities. Much of the decision making depends on the balance sheet and the financial strength of the buyer. But you must know what the deal involves before you start talking price.

I worked with a business owner who thought he had a deal for his company, only to find out that once it was reduced to writing the buyer got all of the assets and he had to pay all of the liabilities. If that deal had gone through, there would have been virtually nothing left for the seller.

Once you have begun to talk price and terms, then it is time to call in the professionals. Let them knock out all of the details and then an attorney will draw up a sales agreement.

6. Enter the Due Diligence Process

There is a period between the acceptance of the sale and the closing. It is the time for the buyer to look over all of the details of the financials and make sure everything is exactly how it was represented. This review is called *due diligence*. Deals are often specified to be contingent upon the resolution of the due diligence process. There are often exceptions written into the sales agreement that allow for adjustments depending on the age of receivables, the condition of inventory, or the actual value of sales contracts. Some of these items may be subjective and very aggressive buyers may very well argue each item.

Once you have made the sale, you may be less resistant to the pressure of a buyer who tries to lower the price based on everything he or she checks. Make sure the sales agreement covers as much as possible and watch out for this technique. A buyer who has done many deals may use this strategy to lower the purchase price by 10%-20%. With one of my clients, a buyer dropped an offer of $1.5 million to $1 million two days before closing based on an erroneous interpretation of their agreement. They did not close.

7. Make Sure You Get Paid

One of the most critical elements of your sale is how and when you will see your money. A very experienced buyer will try to buy your business using its own cash flow. You, on the other hand, will want to get as much up front as you can. In the end, you will likely get a little of each.

Some of the deals you may be offered may also include compensation in the form of an employment contract. You may be attracted to this, as it lowers capital gains and perhaps keeps you involved with the company. Remember, though, that you will have no guarantee of the payment beyond the continued operation and success of the company.

If you are selling to a publicly traded company, you may also be offered payment in the form of stock in the acquiring company. It is likely that you will have to hold that stock for a set period of time before you can sell. If the acquisition is successful, you could add to your return; if it isn't, you may lose a great deal. There have been a number of these deals made that did not work at all, even ending in bankruptcy filing, which wiped out all stock value.

The best deal is one that pays a high proportion of the sale price up front and has a short-term payout of the balance. You want to secure a personal guarantee from the buyer and retain a secured interest in the business assets until you are fully paid. You may be required to subordinate to any bank loans the new owner is either assuming or originating.

> *The sales agreement may stipulate a forfeit that the buyer will pay if the sale does not close. After all, it will cost you money and time to get through the dealing phase.*

Once a Company Is in Play, the Environment Changes

Selling out may be the best move you can make or the only move you have left, but give it serious consideration before you go out and shop the company. Once this process begins, your attention will be taken and the operations of your company will change.

When employees realize that ownership may change, some of them may begin to look for new jobs, assuming that their positions will be less secure with new owners. Vendors may be more stringent on credit. Customers may wonder if the transfer of ownership will affect them. There will be a great deal to manage along with finding, meeting, and negotiating with potential buyers. Be prepared for the increase in activity.

Chapter Key Points

- The corporate world gives out golden parachutes and gold watches for retirement. On the other hand, a business owner strikes gold by turning over his or her interest in the company.

- A merger may be the way to bring needed resources into the company and a way to cut back on duties as well.

- A business must be prepared in advance for a merger or a sale.

- You must know the true value of your company in order to accurately set a price.

- A business broker can save time and increase activity, but the cost may be high.

- The deal isn't done until all of the money is paid.

EPILOGUE: NO SILVER BULLETS

If you have been reading this book hoping that you will find a silver bullet within its pages, you must realize by now that you are out of luck. Think back to the days when you were starting out: it certainly wasn't an easy task, but one worth the sacrifices. And the same holds true now: completing a successful turnaround is a long and arduous process, but one surely worth the effort. The difference between the early days and now is that you began full of energy and promise and now you are probably worn down and filled to the brim with frustration.

But be assured that there is hope: you absolutely can be successful in bringing your company back to health and vibrancy. After all, you have resources to draw on—employees, customers, vendors, and associates. It is in everyone's best interest to see you once again prosperous—jobs will be saved, bills will be paid, and customers will have the choice and service they desire. Continue to work hard, be honest about your dealings, and, in just a few months, your business life will begin getting easier. Once the immediate pressure is relieved, you'll see your optimism return.

I understand that it isn't easy to reach out to family, friends, and associates for the help you need. You may be feeling a loss of confidence in your own ability or even anger at which has happened around you. Maybe your problems are the result of the failure of the general economy or maybe a specific group of customers created most of your difficulty. It would be all too easy to spend your time and energy on placing blame for how you got here. Instead, you'll need to focus your attention on how you're going to correct the situation. Virtually every small business faces critical problems at least once. The issue here isn't that you hit the wall; the issue is how you come off the wall.

A word here about trying to redress the actions of others through lawsuits. Perhaps what happened to you was the result of the illegal acts of another company. It is reasonable to want to take action: you hope that a court or a jury will make you whole. While that may happen eventually, it is highly unlikely to come in time to cure the problems you are currently experiencing. You must make the decision whether you can go forward without the proceeds or other corrections you are demanding in your legal case or whether you want to close up and pursue the case. Don't wait and hope that it will all change sometime soon. It won't.

There are a number of very successful entrepreneurs who have been down at one time in their careers. Even the legendary Donald Trump went through some forced restructuring. It isn't the easiest way to learn, but it is guaranteed that you will learn. Success does not teach as well. You will come out of this smarter and stronger.

Your business will not be the same as it was once this process is over—and neither will you. Your decision will be whether this is still a good match for you. In my case, I decided that it wasn't.

SECOND WIND

In the 1980s, I went through it all—a complicated lawsuit and a complete restructuring of my manufacturing business. In the end, I no longer enjoyed the work and knew that would eventually reflect in how I was managing my company. So I sold it and moved on. After 21 years at it, my life changed drastically. But I did not regret it for a moment. It is a tough call to make.

It takes courage to tackle new risks on top of those that haven't worked out as you expected. I respect you for making the decision to continue the life of the business you may have founded and you still believe in.

I am interested in how your effort has succeeded and welcome any comments you have. You may contact me at the following address:

> Suzanne Caplan
> PGM Group LLC
> PMB 212
> 2927 West Liberty Avenue
> Pittsburgh, PA 15216
> suzcaplan@aol.com

APPENDIX A

BANKRUPTCY

UNDERSTANDING IT

There are three forms of bankruptcy with some use for businesses. Any business owner considering the possibility should seek the advice of an experienced bankruptcy lawyer.

Chapter 7—Liquidation

A Chapter 7 filing almost always ends the operating life of the business. In a very few cases, the business will continue to operate under the supervision of a trustee while an attempt is made to sell it as a going concern.

In most Chapter 7 filings, once the papers have been submitted to the court, a trustee is appointed and all business assets are turned over to his or her control. That means everything, including cash, inventory, equipment, and real estate. If there are any secured lenders who have claim to assets, those may be passed to their control.

All assets will be liquidated and all receivables collected so that everything is reduced to cash. Then, there will be a distribution to all creditors according to their standing. Wages and taxes will be paid before vendor credit that is unsecured. One of the concerns is that assets are sold quickly and at a price far below their value and creditors are paid very little. In some cases, former owners may still be liable to pay the shortage.

Chapter 11—Reorganization

The most typical business filing, Chapter 11 may be initiated through either a voluntary petition, filed by the debtor, or an involuntary petition, filed by creditors that meet certain requirements. Chapter 11 allows the company to continue operating and take some time to propose a plan to repay the creditors. During this time, no action can be taken against the company without permission of the court.

The initial period that allows the debtor the exclusive right to propose a plan is 120 days, a period that the debtor may exceed with the permission of the court. After the period has expired, a creditor or the case trustee may file a plan.

Any plan is proposed that must include a classification of claims and specify how creditors in each class will be treated:

- *Administrative*—any unpaid wages, some union benefits, all professional fees incurred during the cases, and all new debts such as vendor credit or unpaid taxes—must be paid upon confirmation.
- *Secured debt* is paid in full according to agreement with each creditor.
- *Unsecured priority debt*—the unpaid payroll and property taxes—must be paid within 70 months at full value.
- *Unsecured debt*—primarily vendor credit—is paid back on a percentage of face value over a period of 72 months.

The problems are the cost of professional fees added to

the debt and the pressure of the paperwork required. Only one in five companies is successfully reorganized.

Chapter 13—Individual Debt Adjustment

This bankruptcy filing is most often used to pay personal debts. It is not normally used in a business situation, because the payment plan requires a guaranteed wage or income. However, in some cases when there is part-time employment, when a spouse works, or where there is investment income, Chapter 13 can provide relief for business owners. Any individual, even if self-employed or operating an unincorporated business, is eligible for Chapter 13 if his or her debts are below a certain limit.

Any person filing for Chapter 13 must provide the following information:

- a list of all creditors and the amounts and nature of their claims
- the source, amount, and frequency of his or her income
- a list of all of his or her property
- a detailed list of monthly living expenses

All debts are paid by the plan, which usually covers a period of 36-60 months. The plan also pays even most current obligations, including mortgage payments. A regular payment will be submitted to the Chapter 13 trustee, whose office will be make disbursements. Failure to pay will cause dismissal of the filing, although in some instances a modification can be made.

APPENDIX B

CASE STUDY: A SMALL CONSTRUCTION COMPANY STAGES A COMEBACK

FINDING A WAY OUT

Bill King (not his real name) has been an electrician since he was a teenager. After high school and a few years in the service, he got a union card and a full-time job. From almost the beginning, he also worked on the side for private customers totally unrelated to the work he did for his employer. They were manufacturers and Bill and the rest of his department installed and maintained equipment.

Occasionally Bill was asked to do a job that required more than he could accomplish in a reasonable time. He would recruit some of the men he worked with and they would share the fee for the job. This started his business, a company named King Electric.

For years, Bill earned less than 10% of his annual income from his company. But in the early '70s, a large general contractor approached Bill about becoming a regular subcontractor on his projects. It sounded like a great opportunity and Bill accepted. He hired four union electricians on a full-time basis and convinced his wife to keep the books. He kept his job, just in case. The company made money and grew over the next five years. Finally, Bill also became full time. Revenues grew gradually, but always profitably.

SECOND WIND

A year after Bill left his job, one of his former coworkers called to tell him the company was bidding out a very large job and suggested Bill knew more than others about what was involved and he should bid. This one project was twice as large as annual revenues had been, but Bill didn't hesitate. The company was on its way.

Bill hired more employees, purchased new equipment and trucks, and began looking for a formal business location: the company needed real space to park vehicles and store inventory. On the basis of the new contract, Bill borrowed money to finance everything. King Electric continued to grow, never making big profits but always paying its bills.

In the mid-'90s, Bill decided to put the push on to grow. The company had never bid on government projects, but now Bill decided they were ready for this work. But they weren't—and it almost destroyed the whole company.

First, their lack of estimation experience meant that they underbid a good bit of the work and were awarded the contracts as the low bidder. In the best of outcomes, they were likely to lose money on most of their work. Add to that their lack of sophistication about getting paperwork on extras and how their cash flow would be affected by the retainage (payment withheld until approval of a completed project) and the losses mounted with every year. They were not paying vendors and were beginning to get behind in their union payments as well.

The bookkeeping system did not keep up and seldom if ever took collection action. The older and more profitable clients were being lost in all of the panic about what was happening to the company.

We Begin the Process

When I first met the Kings, they described their major problem as cash flow: some bigger projects had not paid timely and their bank balances were dangerously low. Many payrolls were absolute nightmares: they often held their own checks and sometimes had to deposit their own money to cover. Banks that wanted to lend a few years ago were no longer as friendly. They were working harder than ever and continuing to lose ground.

My first task was to show them what was happening. It required a higher level of financial knowledge: they had to understand cost accounting. It didn't matter at this point if they had collected every dollar, because they were losing money on many of their current jobs. The Kings and their managers needed to understand this before we could begin to take action to correct and then change this circumstance.

The Company Stabilizes

It was decided by consensus that no new contracts would be sought until we could determine where the problem areas were and we could correct them. Cash was precariously low and that had to be corrected immediately with aggressive collection action. In a few cases, in order to get paid, we settled disputes over extra charges.

The slowing down of large contract bidding resulted in a cutback of workers as well as administrative staff. We called vendors and asked for time to develop payment arrangements. Payroll was now manageable and that took a good bit of the pressure off so the Kings could focus on raising a bit of cash. To create a backup fund, they sold excess equipment that was not being used, including a crane truck sitting in their yard, and much of their unnecessary inventory. They were establishing control.

The Kings and two of their long-time managers agreed to a 20% pay cut for a period of 90 days. It was expected that losses would be stopped by that time and cash flow would be positive.

An In-Depth Review of the Operations

I wasn't surprised that a complete review of contracts—present as well as recently completed—proved that only one had made a small profit. But it shocked the principals that only one job came in at breakeven. The rest had lost money: a few losses were fairly substantial and one job still in progress was already seriously in the red. Without the recent cash infusion from asset sales (most of the items had been expensed), the company would have been seriously insolvent.

We took a serious look at the way they were costing their estimates. They were not accounting for many of the fixed overhead costs. In addition, and possibly more serious, was the absence of cost allocation and review while a contract in progress. If the material purchased or labor used exceeded what had been projected, no one was monitoring this problem in order to correct it before serious overruns happened. The answer to this has become much easier in recent years: much of the off-the-shelf accounting software has cost tracking abilities that are easier to set up and give excellent reports. We began tracking jobs immediately.

The next step was to look at some overhead items that seemed excessive. The cost of insurance had grown by almost 40% in less than three years. The Kings had the same agent for all of this time and they did not do much of a review of their coverage or the premium costs. This was a mistake, as this agent spent no time trying to control costs, since he thought he had the business no matter what he did. A call to other agents for quotes ended up with almost 20% savings from the original broker.

Another area that had grown out of control was telephone service. It seemed as if everyone had a cell phone and most had two-way radios as well. In addition, phones that had been lost were replaced but never turned off. Using a new service that replaced two pieces of equipment with one and discontinued those not in service, we made a dramatic cut in costs—almost 50%.

Our final area of analysis came in the billing procedures, checking whether or not they were billing timely, capturing all of the extras, and generating all of the paperwork needed to complete the contracts and release held retainage. The upgraded software and a more disciplined office procedure was the key to this effort. When this work began, King Electric was still waiting for final retainage payments on three completed contracts. With a profit margin of 12%-15%, if everything went perfectly, and a 10% retainage, all of the money they needed to go forward was still outstanding.

Implementing Change

While they were focusing their attention on making things stable, they were making no major decisions. They were only bidding sporadically on jobs for which there was a high degree of confidence in their ability to complete as requested. These were for contractors they knew well and involved work that was fairly straightforward. They were not quoting any complicated wiring systems that they hadn't done before.

They kept the chief estimator busy by assigning him the task of reviewing work in progress. Still, he was costing more than the value of his job. And the current thinking was that they would pull back from the larger public contract work that seemed to have caused most of the problems. Sadly, after three years of hard work and loyalty, the estimator was released. Everyone walked around with a long face for days. This was the beginning of other strong actions.

When one of the more difficult big jobs ended, the supervisor from that job also was laid off. In other times, he would have been reassigned to any available work, even though his pay scale was too high to cover, because they wanted him available for the next big project. Other personnel changes were made—including one important new hire.

The time had long since come to hire a full-time bookkeeper/office manager. The company had been keeping the books too casually and missing vital information and important danger signs. Even though the company was using a computer, no one was looking at reports beyond the bank balance and the listing of accounts receivable and payable. The Kings agreed that they needed to look at profitability on a monthly basis.

They sold several trucks that were no longer in use and returned one truck on lease to the dealer, who arranged that it could be traded for a vehicle the Kings needed. This saved money in insurance, upkeep, and gas.

They had to renegotiate the bank loan as well. Some of the cash that came in from the sale of trucks and equipment was used to pay down the balance and then they took a larger mortgage on the building, extending out the payments. Debt service quickly became easier to manage.

The toughest decision to be made was about the work to be bid as the company went further. Originally Bill King was excited about building a multimillion-dollar business; that dream did not just go away. He did not readily accept the idea of shrinking the company in order to save it. I worked for weeks with the new office manager and the company accountant to create pro formas that showed how the company was likely to perform under various business models. A small company with mostly industrial projects either billed on time and material or quoted was the most profitable. No one closed the door on large projects, but we all agreed the risk had to be worth the reward.

They instituted entirely new work habits as well, with regular meetings scheduled to discuss the progress of all of the work. Instead of doing it on the fly, Bill King, his sons who were working for the company, and all job supervisors came into the office once a week. They listened to reports and gave each other advice. More often than not, the new bookkeeper was there as well, giving updates about total material costs on each project and labor costs to date. Everyone benefited from this change.

Final Step: Future Plans

For almost two years, everyone at King Electric was working as hard as they could just to keep the company alive. After six months of getting things under control, we began to discuss what was next.

The Kings agreed along the way about the big projects, but every time we received a new invitation to bid, they wanted to discuss it again. You could see in the boys' faces that they were not very anxious to get in over their heads any time soon. So we found a workable compromise. Another electrical contracting company that had just started doing large municipal construction work called to borrow some equipment and that began a conversation about the problems of growing and taking on big jobs. Bill King was an open, honest man and that seemed to impress his friendly competition. In less than two weeks, I was invited to sit in on an idea session they decided to have.

Even before this meeting, I had thought that a joint venture would be an interesting idea. Less equipment and labor would be needed on a day-to-day basis, but could be called upon when the pressure was on to finish a phase of the project. Too much money was lost being overstaffed when it wasn't necessary. They decided to try a small project together and it worked well. The two companies have been looking for a large project to share.

Both of the Kings were worn out from the events of the past few years. Only in their early 60s, they were now considering selling out. It wasn't what they really wanted, but both were sure they couldn't survive the pressure of another downturn. The boys seldom gave an opinion on this topic.

Succession had been Bill King's original intention; that was really the motivation for trying to build up a large company. He learned that cash flow did not replace profits, so it was unclear to him how to try and pass the company on. The boys weren't sure they wanted it, given what they had experienced.

It was decided that the next two years would be spent in trying to rebuild the financial base of the business. No buyers would be sought and some experimentation on transition would begin. The Kings would take two three-week vacations, leaving the sons in charge, and they would all monitor how that worked. Their accountant also was going to work on setting a value for the business.

This experience had taken a toll on all of the Kings: they were all a bit less enthusiastic about the construction business than they had been a few years ago. But, they were all more knowledgeable and that was beginning to encourage them as well. The senior Kings felt as if they understood what mistakes they had made and wouldn't repeat them. The sons had been talking among themselves about how they would further change the operation. It's not an easy way to learn, but one that definitely makes an impression.

APPENDIX C

ADVICE FROM PROFESSIONALS

AN ATTORNEY, A BANKER, A CPA, AND A TURNAROUND SPECIALIST

An Attorney's Perspective

Alan Cech is a lawyer in Pittsburgh, Pennsylvania, and a graduate of the University of Pittsburgh School of Law. Mr. Cech is in private practice, focusing on business organizations, workouts, and commercial litigation.

The businesspeople who enter their lawyer's office may look and dress differently from one another. They may harbor different notions and attitudes as to what brought them to the point of seeking legal help. By and large, however, their differences are outnumbered by their similarities.

The following is typical of situations that confront the attorney.

The Situation

Mr. Smith has run his own company, a small tool and die manufacturing company, for 20 years. For the first 15 years, Mr. Smith made a good living and looked forward to bringing his two sons into the business.

Five years ago, Mr. Smith started bidding on larger industrial projects, which had a greater profit potential. To handle the larger projects, he moved his company to a new location, added employees, and purchased new equipment. At the same time, Mr. Smith took out a large line of credit loan to pay for all of the changes.

The bank, in order to ensure that Mr. Smith would pay the line of credit, had Mr. Smith's wife, two sons, and their wives co-sign the loan. In addition, the bank placed liens on all of the company's assets and mortgages on the homes of Mr. Smith and both of his sons.

Business did not go as expected and, for the first time in his experience, the company was unable to pay its creditors on time. In order to keep his creditors happy, Mr. Smith obtained yet another loan from the bank, pledging as collateral all of the assets not already pledged to the bank, including his wife's retirement money.

Because the loan did nothing to improve his business's profitability, however, revenues continued to decline. In order to keep the mortgages current, Mr. Smith started to use the tax monies he had withheld from his employees' wages and paid those creditors who made his life the most miserable (although not the ones most important to his survival).

Now What?

As Mr. Smith sits in his attorney's conference room, he is faced with the threat of tax levies (not to mention criminal prosecution) for failing to pay withholding taxes, he has no capital or lending source to meet operating expenses, the bank has started foreclosure on his and his sons' homes, and the process server is serving him with a new lawsuit every day. More important, Mr. Smith just doesn't know what to do next. From his lawyer he wants one thing, and one thing only: "Make them stop!"

What most clients do not appreciate is that, while it is possible to "make them stop" for at least a little while, it will do nothing to make things better, it will do nothing to improve the business, and it will serve only to waste remaining cash and personal resources on unnecessary legal action.

Too many times the attorney will not see the entire picture and will believe that the lawsuits are real disputes, rather than collection actions. Other times, the attorney will engage in costly litigation because it is what the client wants and because he or she can bill hourly for the work. And still other times, the attorney will engage in litigation to give his or her client "breathing room" without having a plan for what to do with that time.

It is important to remember that, more often than not, a business failure is brought about by business concerns, not legal concerns. And because of that, the solution is not in legal recourse but in the application of sound business practices.

This is not to say that a lawyer is unnecessary. A lawyer is an essential part of the turnaround team. The lawyer should not, however, be the focal point of the turnaround team.

Advice

So, what should your lawyer do?

- Your lawyer should put you in touch with a competent business consultant with experience in turnarounds, if you have not already found one.
- Your lawyer should stop actions and/or lawsuits by creditors or—at the very least—delay those lawsuits while a turnaround plan is being devised and implemented.
- Your lawyer should consult with the turnaround team regarding liens, mortgages, and tax obligations so as to understand the relative bargaining power of each creditor.
- Your lawyer should prepare for filing a reorganization (Chapter 11) bankruptcy, should it become necessary.

- Your lawyer should negotiate and document "standstill agreements" (agreements forestalling litigation) and payment arrangements—and, when appropriate, coerce, threaten, and intimidate troublesome creditors in order to keep them in line and to work with you during the turnaround.

Not all attorneys (or all clients) will follow this approach. Why not? Many attorneys want to "take the lead" and provide business as well as legal advice. Sometimes they do not want to share available funds with a business consultant. More often, clients will let pride get in the way and refuse to consult someone about how they might run their business more profitably. Legal advice is one thing; business advice is another.

A turnaround requires an assortment of skills, properly managed and properly utilized. The lawyer is crucial only as part of the overall plan.

A Banker's Perspective

Tom Nunnally is Senior Relationship Manager at Enterprise Bank in Pittsburgh. Formerly the President of Iron and Glass Bank, Tom is also the co-author of The Small Business Insider's Guide to Banks *(Oasis Press/PSI Research, 1997).*

There are often times when a business has an adverse circumstance that jeopardizes the ability to service debt. This can come in the form of profit margins that are not met, a downturn in sales, or the failure of large trade creditor to pay on time or at all.

The first thing that a borrower must realize, in its relationship with a bank (or even trade creditors and landlords), is that this is not an uncommon event. Rarely in life do things happen just as we have planned them. So there is no great shame in visiting with the bank to discuss the adverse turn of events.

Where there is great shame, and a severe loss of credibility, is in keeping these circumstances from a bank, either by withholding information or by outright misrepresentation.

A banker will have clues that things are not going right—overdrafts, the failure to get financial statements as promised, and finally late payments. So you can fool some of the creditors some of the time, but not all of the time. By waiting to inform the lender, you are just digging a bigger hole from which to climb.

By the way, it is never a good idea to borrow from others who are not willing participants, such as stretching out the trade payables (beyond terms) or failing to pay withholding taxes. The latter causes big problems, in that it not only is expensive, but also makes any lender very suspect of the borrower's business savvy.

And a borrower should not open and use an account at another bank to keep funds away from the primary lender. If a dialogue is not forthcoming, then the lender (especially a large bank) may transfer the loan to a workout department (for liquidation). The people staffing this area usually do not have the authority or the mission to restructure the debt; their mission is to terminate it. It is in the borrower's best interest to stay out of this department, so the workout should begin quickly (and hopefully remain) with the current loan officer.

A borrower should realize that this is now not business as usual and be willing to make certain adjustments to the operation of the business (and personal lifestyle) if the business is worth saving. If not, early recognition can save much anguish and money, as the borrower will maximize the cash to liquidate debt and avoid a shortfall that he or she may have to cover through his or her guarantee.

The first step is for the borrower to meet with the lender, with a plan in hand to turn the cash flow around.

Even if this is only a concept, the borrower should be proactive in the plan and not wait for the lender to come up with a solution. The borrower's plan may not be feasible in its initial concept, but it is a starting place for the lender to suggest what he or she may be willing to do.

The most practical solution for a lender is to grant an extension of the time to repay. This might be in the form of interest only on a term loan for a period of time. It might also include a longer period to repay the debt. If the situation is temporary, this may be sufficient action, if taken early, to put the ship back on course.

If there are losses that eat into working capital, then there may be a need for more money to replenish the working capital. There are four ways to replenish capital: future profits, borrowing, sale of assets, and equity injection.

If the turnaround has started, then the borrower may be able to convince the lender that the future profits can restore the minimum working capital. This may be through correcting the root problem or a new contract.

The lender may not be willing or able to grant more money unless there are "undermargined" assets or additional (outside) collateral available. If the assets are already utilized to the maximum, the lender will probably prefer to take a loss on the balance now, rather than a larger loss later. And additional debt is not always the answer to a problem; the root of the problem is what should be addressed.

In some cases, a lender will release collateral (especially assets not essential to the operation of the business) or permit others to lend on that collateral (those that can comfortably grant a higher loan-to-value percentage).

During the turnaround process, the borrower should be open-minded: termination or sale of the business should always be an option to be continually considered, even if distasteful to the borrower. There should be frequent and timely discussions between the banker and the borrower.

Keep in mind that the lender will be under some pressure from the federal banking regulators to keep them abreast of the situation and progress. And if the borrower does not keep the communications flowing and make some progress, the regulators have the power to order a charge-off (and the subsequent recovery).

During problem times, the borrower should keep cool, keep communicating, and keep promises.

A Certified Public Accountant's Perspective

David M. Wilke, CPA, MBA, is the founding partner of Wilke & Associates, LLP, a small business advisory Certified Public Accounting firm in Pittsburgh, Pennsylvania. David was named the 1997 Western Pennsylvania Accounting Advocate of the Year by the Small Business Administration. Wilke & Associates may be reached at www.wilkecpa.com and at 877 208-2200.

Why did I fail? How did I lose money? What steps can I take to prevent failure? When will I reach my breakeven point? Do I have any choices? Where will I be in five years?

Small business owners often ask themselves these questions and, for a variety of reasons, they choose not to discover the answers. The answers to these questions can be found in a business plan, particularly the financial statement projections.

Example 1

Let's pretend 10 small business owners each have a one-year performance contract with Nike Shoes. The terms of the contract allow for a $100,000 payment to each owner based on his or her performance for one full year. The performance requirement is a simple marketing task for the

SECOND WIND

Nike Web site. Every morning for an entire year, each owner needs to successfully tie two running shoes on his or her feet within one minute from start to finish.

Through our experiences with small business owners, we expect the following to occur:

- Three small business owners will break their shoelaces during the year and fail.
- One small business owner will break his hand and fail.
- Two small business owners will forget to wear shoes with laces and fail.
- One small business owner will get so nervous that he will run out of time to complete the task and fail.
- The remaining three small business owners will document and track every completed day and count the remaining days until the goal is achieved. They will carry at least three backup shoelaces just in case the laces break, they will practice tying their shoes using their teeth and feet in the event of a hand injury, and they will hire two companies to remind them daily to tie their shoes. Lastly, they will practice every day for two weeks before the contract begins, so they will have confidence in their ability to tie their shoes within one minute. These are the small business owners who will receive $100,000.

Achieving an extremely simple goal is impossible without a good plan and a complete backup procedure. Proper planning and organization is the difference between success and failure. In the Nike example, business owners who planned for expected problems were successful, while those who did not failed.

Example 2

By analyzing the true story of a small landscaping business with revenues of approximately $1,000,000, we can see how planning and proper utilization of professionals may have prevented a bankruptcy.

The story of our landscaping company is similar to the stories of many small businesses. The company started small and grew over a period of 10 years to over one million in sales. As revenues increased, the owner spent less time with billing and bill-paying issues. He was busy selling to new customers and managing projects. They were excellent landscapers; however, the owner wanted to add general contracting services to complement the landscaping business, at the request of some customers.

The owner accepted a $50,000 contracting job and, due to many problems with getting the job done on time and correctly, the contract was disputed and not paid. The landscaper did not have a backup plan for this problem and began to use payroll tax money and sales tax money to pay wages and vendors on time. He was unable to pay his bank loan. Instead of discussing these problems with his banker and accountant, the owner attempted to sell more contracting services and, unfortunately, lost more money.

The owner did not have a plan and did not have accurate monthly financial statements to show the losses in the contracting business and the profits in the landscaping business. The bank loans were secured by the owner's personal residence and the bank and the IRS proceeded with collection activity that forced the owner to file bankruptcy to avoid losing his home and his business. The bankruptcy attorney required a retainer of $15,000 in order to start the bankruptcy proceeding. The amazing thing was that the owner was able to pay this retainer.

The irony is that if the owner had invested $5,000 in a business plan and accurate accounting records before he jumped into the contracting business, he might have avoided bankruptcy. Most businesses do not survive a bankruptcy; however, our landscaper has reorganized under Chapter 11 of the United States Bankruptcy Code and is profitable today. The total legal and accounting costs through the bankruptcy process were about $45,000. The reputation of the business has been damaged, to some degree. On the other hand, the owner has learned some valuable lessons: he will always have accurate accounting records, he has a business plan with projections, and he discusses all major business decisions with his accountant. The "cookie jar" money that was used in this bankruptcy could have been used to prevent the bankruptcy.

Recommendations

As a small business owner, you must know and accept your weaknesses—and you must develop a plan to protect against them. In the case above, the owner was evidently weak with general contracting services, but did the work anyway.

As CPAs we have seen many business failures and many business successes. To avoid failure, the business owner must be careful of the following deadly sins:

- No business plan
- Not enough profitable sales
- Growing too fast with too little capital
- No cash deficiency safety nets, such as an unused line of credit
- No insurance
- Using payroll or sales tax money to pay bills
- Poor credit policies and poor collections

- No financial information/budgets/tracking
- Not adapting to industry change
- No contingency plans/backup plan

Use your CPA as your coach and trainer. Don't buy "tax compliance" as a commodity. Use the person who knows you and your business intimately as an advisor—not just as a tax preparer. Often a small business owner thinks of his or her CPA as another "expense" or an "overhead cost." Sometimes small business owners try to minimize this cost and, in effect, discourage the strategies and ideas inside the mind of their trusted advisor.

When you plan to succeed, you most likely will succeed. When you document your goals and dreams, they become real. When you act like a winner, you are a winner. The motivational writer Og Mandino says to "never, never, never, never quit," for if you quit you have guaranteed failure.

A Turnaround Consultant's Perspective

Patrick Wisman, CTP, is a principal in Preferred Business Solutions, LLC, a national turnaround firm. He is a Certified Turnaround Professional (CTP), a designation of the Turnaround Management Association.

Approach to Companies in Distress

When my partners and I are asked to aid a company in distress, we look for three success requirements:

1. Is there a core business or businesses?
2. Does the company possess the human resources to accomplish a turnaround?
3. Does the company have the capital or access to capital needed to do the turnaround?

The answers to these three questions determine the

nature of our involvement. We will be advising, performing as interim management, or a combination of both and maybe trying to raise capital. However, if there isn't a core business, it is most likely a liquidation.

If it is determined that the company is a candidate for a turnaround, it will go through five predictable stages:

- Management Change
- Situation Analysis
- Emergency Action
- Business Restructuring
- Return to "New" Normal

The events that take place in each of these stages in financial, marketing, operations, organization, etc. are predictable. By constantly monitoring, you are able to tell where you are in the process.

The first stage, Management Change, is the reality check for all involved. It is the stage where you select the top management team and work out the impediments to success. This can and most likely will include replacing some managers. It is then that owners reveal whether or not they are committed to change. If they are, they most likely will be successful.

GLOSSARY OF TERMS

Accounts Payable represent a company's outstanding debts to vendors. A listing of accounts payable is normally compiled alphabetically and the entries are made by the date of the invoice. The total of these invoices is shown on the balance sheet as a liability. Vendor credit may be a significant portion of working capital, so due dates must be tracked for payment. Some suppliers charge a penalty if not paid within certain terms. At the end of each month, accounts payable should be aged in a report showing amount due on a 30-, 60-, and 90-day basis.

Accounts Payable Turnover is calculated by dividing the total of credit purchases by the current total of accounts payable. This number may be divided into 365 to give the average number of days it takes the company to pay a vendor invoice.

Accounts Receivable represent the money due from all customers currently owing at least one invoice to the company. The total of these invoices is shown on the balance sheet as an asset. Accounts receivable should be aged in a report similar to one described in *accounts payable* at the end of each month as they represent expected incoming cash flow.

Accounts Receivable Turnover is calculated by dividing the total of credit sales by the current total of accounts receivable. This number may be divided into 365 to give the average number of days required to turn a sale (including credit) into cash. Accounts receivable turnover is a benchmark number for measuring the effectiveness of collection policy.

Accrual Basis Accounting is a system that recognizes income at the time a sale is made, rather than when payment is received, and expense at the time it is incurred, rather than when it is paid. Income and expense are matched during a fixed accounting period, allowing for accurate comparisons.

Accrued Expenses are those expenses that are anticipated although not yet due, such as tax incurred during one period and due at a later time. Other payroll costs, such as earned vacation, may also be reported when accrued. This produces a more accurate statement of the financial condition of the business.

Accrued Income (Accrued Revenue) is any income earned during an accounting period but not received by the end of it.

Amortization is the process of allocating a portion of the total amount of an item over a fixed period. For example, if the start-up expense is substantial, you may expense it over a fixed period of time. The total cost of an acquisition will be allocated over the life of the project.

Assets represent the values of any tangible property and property rights less any reserves set aside for depreciation. Assets do not, on the other hand, reflect any appreciation in value unless they are sold for the greater value.

Bad Debts are unpaid obligations that are deemed uncollectible after a series of collection activities. Bad debts are normally written off on an annual basis.

Balance Sheet shows the summary of assets and liabilities of a company. It is created at the end of an accounting period, such as a month, a quarter, or a year. Subtracting liabilities from assets shows the net worth of the business. Assets are listed as current or fixed and liabilities are listed as current or long term.

Bankruptcy is a legal state of insolvency. A company deemed to be in this condition may choose protection under the law to allow a chance to reorganize (Chapter 11) or liquidate in an orderly fashion (Chapter 7). For details, see Appendix A.

Book Value is the value of any asset shown on the balance sheet. It is determined by the item's cost and then reduced by the amount of depreciation. The book value of an item does not necessarily reflect its current market value. Accelerated depreciation may reduce the value below market.

Bulk Transfer is a regulation under the Uniform Commercial Code that covers the sale and transfer of more than 50% of a company's assets. Under this article, notification of all creditors is required in advance of completion of such a sale. This is meant to prevent any fraud from taking place in a business sale.

Business Plan is a written document describing the nature of the business, the sales and marketing strategy, and the financial background, and containing a projected profit and loss statement. Originally written as a strategic plan for a new business, it should be updated every year and revamped every three years.

Capital is the liquid worth of a company, often determined by the total of all assets less any outstanding liabilities.

Cash Basis Accounting is a system that recognizes income only when payment is received and expenses only when payment is made. This works best for a business where most transactions are done with cash instead of credit. There is no match of revenue against expense in a fixed accounting period, so comparisons of previous periods are not possible. There is less financial control in a cash basis system than in an accrual basis system.

Cash Flow is the difference between the available cash at the beginning of an accounting period and that at the end of a period. Cash comes in from sales, loan proceeds, investments, and the sale of assets and goes out to pay for operating and direct expenses, principal debt service, and the purchase of assets.

Cash Flow Statement measures the inflow of revenue versus the outflow of expense. The most relevant type of cash flow statement is done on an operating basis. You may also include loan proceeds once it has been established that they will be forthcoming.

Chapter 7 Bankruptcy is an option by which a firm is liquidated after the court has determined that reorganization is not worthwhile. A trustee is charged with liquidating all assets and distributing the proceeds to satisfy claims by order of priority. See Appendix A.

Chapter 11 Bankruptcy is an option by a firm reorganizes under the guidance of an appointed trustee. It is expected that the firm will continue operating. See Appendix A.

Chart of Accounts is a numerical listing of all items contained in the financial statement of a company, including assets, liabilities, income, and expense.

Collateral consists of any tangible assets that are pledged and encumbered (subjected to a legal claim) to secure a loan.

Compensating Balances are monies on deposit by the borrower in operating accounts that are maintained by a lender. Certain average balances may be required by the lender to compensate for a special interest rate charged on a loan. Loan fees may also be waived for borrowers who maintain a high level of compensating balances.

Confession of Judgment is a clause used in many contracts, including most loan agreements, that permits the creditor to file a lien against the debtor without filing a suit in court. This clause is normally exercised only when there has been a default in the terms. Only some states allow this clause.

Co-Signer is an additional signer to any financial obligation who is fully obligated to all of the terms of the note until it is paid.

Covenant Not to Compete is an agreement between buyer and seller of a business that prevents the previous owner from competing in a similar business for a specific period of time or a specific geographical area.

Current Assets are assets that are in cash or are expected to be turned into cash within one year, such as inventory and accounts receivable. Current assets will not include any miscellaneous payables such as notes from officers, because there may be no expectation that they will be paid on any specific schedule.

Current Liabilities are debts or costs that are due within one year. These include accounts payable, current portions due of any loans, and any accrued but unpaid expenses (e.g., taxes, insurance, or benefits such as accrued vacation pay).

Current Ratio is current assets divided by current liabilities from the most recent quarter. There should be about twice as many assets as liabilities, for a 2-to-1 ratio, to ensure sufficient cash flow to meet obligations (also called *solvency*).

Debt is money owed to a lender, vendor, service provider, or any other creditor.

Debt Service is the total payment of an obligation, consisting of principal and interest.

Debt-to-Equity Ratio is a measure of the extent to which a firm's capital is provided by owners or lenders, calculated by dividing debt by equity. If ratios are increasing—more debt in relation to equity—the company is being financed by creditors rather than by internal positive cash flow. This may be a dangerous trend.

Depreciation is an expense item set up to express the diminishing life expectancy and value of any equipment (including vehicles). Depreciation is set up over a fixed period of time based on current tax regulations. Items fully depreciated are no longer carried as assets on the company books.

Direct Costs are the costs of material and labor that are directly attributable to the level of sales or production; they may include the costs of direct subcontractors. Direct costs are referred to as *variable* costs because they rise as volume increases and drop as it decreases. Total revenue less direct costs equals the gross profit from operations.

Due Diligence describes a process by which a buyer under contract to purchase a business conducts an investigation into the company's operations and financial condition. Backup documentation is verified and tax and public records are checked for accuracy. Equipment may be scrutinized and a current inventory taken as well. Any discrepancies are often settled as adjustments to the sales price.

Equity, also called *net worth*, is the difference between the total assets of the business and the total liabilities. Shown on the liability side of the balance sheet, equity may be thought of as an amount owed to owners because theoretically it would be disbursed to them if assets were sold and liabilities were paid.

Equity Financing is the strategy of raising capital through an instrument such as stock, which carries ownership risk and reward. Some debt instruments carry convertible features that allow them to be redeemed for stocks. The cost of this capital is higher, since there is risk associated with this type of financing.

Fixed Expenses are the overhead costs that are constant regardless of the level of sales.

Gross Profit is derived from the gross (total before paying taxes) sales revenue less any direct costs such as labor, material, and subcontracting that are directly attributable to those sales. Also referred to as *operating profits*, the gross profit represents the money available to pay overhead expenses and taxes and to generate a net profit for the company to retain as working capital.

Income Statement is a document generated monthly and/or annually that reports the earnings of a company by stating all relevant income and all expenses that have been incurred to generate that income. Also referred to as a *profit and loss statement*.

Indirect Costs are expenses not directly related to sales: items such as rent, utilities, and administrative overhead, including office salaries, professional fees, and selling expenses. Indirect costs are called *overhead* or *fixed expenses* because they continue regardless of the sales level of the company.

Inventory consists of the assets held for sale, which may include finished goods, work in progress, and raw material. When valuing work in progress, the added value of direct labor involved in producing the finished product may increase the real worth of inventory, yet may not be realized until the work is complete and the goods are released to the customer.

Inventory Turnover is a ratio calculated by dividing the total costs of material in costs of goods sold by the current inventory. Decreasing ratios (fewer turnovers per year) may indicate that there are slow-selling items in current inventory that put pressure on the cash position because they will not turn into cash in the current cycle.

Labor Costs are divided into two types—direct and indirect. Direct labor costs are related to producing products and performing services. Indirect labor costs are related to the work involved in distribution, sales, and the administrative duties involved in operating the business. Labor costs include any taxes and benefits due as a result of the payment of wages.

Letter of Credit is an instrument issued by a bank using very specific language to a supplier or vendor with the bank acting as guarantor of an obligation. This instrument is often used in international transactions assuring that once the customers have received the goods they will be remitting payment. This allows a company to import goods without tying up capital while they are in transit.

Liability is money that is owed to a lender or other creditor and is an effect of any owed assets.

Line of Credit is an instrument of credit issued by a bank or other lender for short-term (usually one year) capital needs. Most lines are revolving; that is, they can be drawn down, repaid, and drawn on again. A non-revolving line may be drawn only once. A line of credit should be paid to zero at least once during the year, as its purpose is short-term financing of inventory and receivables. A line of credit is granted for one year, but it may be renewed on a regular basis.

Liquidity is the ability to pay obligations as they become due, using cash on hand or cash generated from the normal turnover (sale) of inventory and from the collection of receivables. Long-term assets (property and equipment) are not considered in liquidity, because they provide no cash from which to retire current debts unless they are sold and become cash items.

Net Profit is the amount of money earned after all expenses (often with the exception of taxes) are deducted.

Net Worth is the amount of equity a company has, which is the difference between the total assets and the total liabilities.

Operating Profits See *gross profit*.

Overhead is the indirect costs or fixed expenses of operating the business, ranging from rent to administrative costs to marketing costs. The majority of these costs stay fixed (the amount is the same from month to month) regardless of sales volume, although a few that are sales-associated may be considered semi-variable.

Payables See *accounts payable*.

Prime Rate is the interest rate that banks charge their best clients (those least likely to default on their loans). It is actually not an official rate set by a government agency. This rate is based on the current federal rate for funds, which goes up and down according to the decisions of the Federal Reserve Board. Banks are free to set their own benchmark rates, but they seldom do so, as most follow the lead of the larger institutions.

Profit and Loss Statement is a statement—often prepared monthly and/or quarterly and always annually—that reports income and expenses and expresses the results as a profit or a loss. The report identifies by category all income, whether from the sales of products or services or from other activities, and all direct and indirect costs. Operating (gross or after-tax) profits are listed as are the net (before tax) profit.

Pro Forma is a preliminary report that may be created as both a profit and loss statement and a cash flow statement. A pro forma for an existing company is a prediction of financial results in future periods, based in part on historical happenings and in part on anticipated new income or expenses. A pro forma is also created for a new enterprise in order to project future capital needs.

Rate of Interest (Fixed or Variable) determines the amount of interest to be paid on a loan and how the loan is paid off. The interest rate that is in effect at the start of a loan may not always be the interest charged throughout the life of the loan. Only a *fixed rate* loan has one rate during the entire term, which normally is limited to five years or less. The only long-term loans that are fixed are mortgages; these loans are sold off through Fannie Mae or Freddie Mac, which relieves the bank of the interest rate risk. A *variable rate* loan has a floating rate pegged to an index, such as the prime rate, and goes up and down according to that index. Some loans may have semi-fixed rates for one year and the rates float, sometimes with a minimum (floor) and/or a maximum (ceiling).

Receivables See *Accounts Receivable*.

Retained Earnings are profits that are not distributed through dividends but are left in the business and carried on the books. This amount is reduced over time by any losses.

Secured Loan is a loan for which the borrower has pledged assets as collateral that the lender may seize and liquidate if the loan is not paid according to the agreement.

Uniform Commercial Code (UCC) is a set of laws governing commercial transactions. When a lender wishes to perfect (protect) its secured interest in certain assets, it may do so in a number of ways. One is to take possession, as with stocks and bonds that are held as security. Another is to file an encumbrance on a title, such as that of a vehicle. Where there are a variety of assets in the possession and control of the borrower, the lender will file a Uniform Commercial Code financing statement with the secretary of state where the borrower is located, in order to establish a lien or priority ownership. These financing statements are normally signed by the borrower at the time the loan closes.

Unsecured Loan is a loan that has no underlying collateral pledged by the borrower to offset any losses to the lender in case of default. An unsecured loan normally carries a higher interest rate than a loan secured by collateral.

Venture Capital consists of funds flowing into a company in the form of an investment rather than a loan. Controlled by an individual or a small group known as *venture capitalists*, these investments require a high rate of return and they are secured by a substantial ownership position in the business. Equity interest transfers back to the original owners when all loan payments and/or premiums are paid.

Working Capital is the difference between current assets and current liabilities; it is an indication of liquidity and the ability of the company to meet current obligations. The assumption is that current assets will turn into cash concurrently with obligations such as payables and loans coming due. The variable here is the collectibility of current receivables and the salability of inventory. Failure of either may mean that a company is less liquid in reality than it appears to be on paper.

Working Capital Ratio is calculated by dividing current assets by current liabilities. A decreasing ratio indicates that working capital is being reduced by losses, such as the purchase of long-term assets or distribution to owners. This ratio may be used to compare your company with peer companies and to monitor trends.

INDEX

A

Accountants, 62–63, 262–266
Accounting systems
    bases, 6
    financial analysis with, 86
    terminology, 7–8
Accrual basis accounting, 6
Accuracy in accounting, 4–5
Across-the-board cuts, 53–54
Add-ons to consultant bills, 162
Administrative cost cutting, 54, 114–115, 117
Administrative fees in bankruptcy, 136, 245
Advance payments on large orders, 31, 78
Advertising
    methods, 109–110
    profitability and, 187–188
Advisory groups
    bringing together, 65–66
    candidates for, 61–62, 65–69
    need for, 60–61
Aegis, 194
Agreements
    with potential buyers of business, 236
    for strategic alliances, 218–221
    succession, 225–227
Airlines
    cost cuts, 50
    employee relations, 74
    equipment leases, 173
    price cuts, 128
    sales volume versus profitability, 93, 188, 208–209
    target markets, 126
Alliances
    examples, 213
    joint product development, 216–217
    in King Electric case study, 253–254
    reasons to create, 211, 214–216
    seeking partners and advice, 217–219
Assets
    assessing value, 138–139
    liabilities versus, 17
    selling to raise cash, 11, 35–36
Associates as advisors, 68–69
Attorneys
    do's and don'ts for, 257–259
    free advice from, 81
    importance when facing bankruptcy, 142–143
    overview of benefits, 63–65
    for strategic alliances, 218–219
Authority
    delegating, 200–201
    passing to next generation, 223–228
Auto leases, 175, 178–179
Automatic stay, 136

B

Bad decisions, avoiding, 42–43
Balance sheets, 139, 235

Balloon payments, 179
Bankers
   as advisors, 66–67
   building relationships with, 19, 34–35
   do's and don'ts for dealing with, 260–262
   renegotiating debt with, 179–181
Bankruptcy
   alternatives, 137–138
   Chapter 7 basics, 136–137
   considering, 132–133
   costs of, 137, 265
   involuntary, 76, 77
   potential Chapter 11 benefits, 134–136
   to stop collection efforts, 180–181
   types, 133–134, 244–246
Barter, 36–37
Bases for accounting systems, 6
Benefits (product), discovering, 107–108
Bidding errors, 248
Blame, avoiding placement of, 22
Blind inquiries, 233
Bonuses, 166, 167
Bookkeepers, 252, 253
Borrowing from friends, 69
Breakeven, 91–92
Budgets, 198–200
Business brokers, 233, 235–236
Business environment, examining, 17
Businesses
   creating image, 194–195
   selling, 140–141, 223–228, 229, 233–239
   valuing, 234
Business owners. *See* Owners
Business plans
   importance, 263–265
   revising, 148
   for strategic alliances, 219–220
Buy-sell agreements, 227

C

Cancellation policies, with consultants, 165
Capital base
   deterioration as danger sign, 11
   rebuilding, 210–211, 261
Car leases, 175, 178–179

Case study: King Electric, 247–255
Cash basis accounting, 6
Cash cushions, 28–29
Cash flow. *See also* Cost cutting
   danger signs, 11
   importance, 28–29
   profitability versus, 130, 208–209
   projecting, 52
   required for growth, 208
   six steps to increase, 29–37
Cech, Alan, 256
Certified public accountants, 262–266
Challenge, examining desire for, 19–20
Change
   preparing for, 21–23
   wrong reasons to seek, 44–45
Chapter 7 bankruptcy, 134, 136–137, 244
Chapter 11 bankruptcy
   costs of, 137, 265
   overview, 133–134, 245
   potential benefits, 134–136
   to stop collection efforts, 180–181
Chapter 13 bankruptcy, 133, 246
Children, communicating with, 79
Cleanup, 235
Clearance sales, 191
Closely held companies, succession plans.
   See Succession plans
Collateral, releasing, 262. *See also* Security
Colleagues as advisors, 68–69
Collections
   communicating to avoid, 74–75
   hiring attorneys for protection against, 64
   renegotiating loans to end, 180–181
   by taxing authorities, 13
   tightening policies, 27, 29–30
Combined purchasing power, 232
Combined services, 232
Communication
   with creditors, 74–77
   with employees, 72–74, 167–168
   with family and friends, 79–80
   target groups, 72
Competitive energy, 19–20

Competitors
    comparing sales and marketing costs
        with, 116
    influence on pricing, 127–128
    selling unprofitable lines to, 189–190
Confidentiality agreements, 219, 236
Consignment agreements, 181
Consolidating companies, 231
Consolidating loans, 63
Consultants
    potential benefits, 156–157
    selecting, 160–162
    sources for, 157–160
    working with, 162–165, 267–268
Contract loans, 208
Contracts
    with consultants, 165
    enforcing, 220–221
    as limitation on cost cutting, 119
Co-signers, 257
Co-sponsors, 215
Cost cutting. *See also* Cash flow; Overhead costs
    across the board, 53–54
    administrative expenses, 54, 114–115, 117
    airline example, 50
    debt, 120–123
    legal restrictions on, 119
    personal expenses, 58
    planning approach to, 123
    setting goals for, 51–53
    vendor cooperation, 56–57
    wages and salaries, 54–56
Cost of goods, 89
Cost per customer, 116
Cost per order, 117
Cost per transaction, 116
Cost tracking, 250
Creditors
    communications with, 74–77
    renegotiating with, 32–33
Criminal prosecution, for overdue taxes, 13, 257
Current assets, 17

Current liabilities, 17
Customer databases, 193
Customer profiles, 107
Customers
    changes in, 106–107
    communications with, 77–78
    continuing to develop, 150–151
    employee treatment of, 73–74
    examining resources to serve, 18
    failures as danger sign, 14
    gathering marketing data about, 106–109
    notifying of discontinued products, 193–194
    requesting down payments from, 31, 78
    sales costs per, 116–117
    sharing optimism with, 148–149
    ways to attract, 109–110

D
Danger signals, 10–15
Databases, 193, 217
Debt. *See also* Bankruptcy; Loans
    effect on solvency, 138–139
    handling in succession plans, 226
    personal liability, 257, 265
    renegotiating, 75, 179–181
    reviewing, 95, 120–123
Debt restructuring
    in Chapter 11 bankruptcy, 135–136, 245
    steps in, 101–102
Decisions, impulsive, 42–43
Delegation, 200–201, 225
Delinquent loans, renegotiating, 180–181. *See also* Debt; Loans
Demand, examining, 17
Demographic checklists, 107
Deposits on large orders, 31, 78
Desert Storm, 123
Desire to compete, 19–20
Development authorities, 159
Differentiation, influence on pricing, 127–128
Direct costs, 7, 126
Discount terms, 30, 128–129
Diversification, 232–233

Down payments on large orders, 31, 78
Due diligence, 237–238

E

E-commerce, 150
Employees. *See also* Morale
    as advisors, 67–68
    communications with, 72–74
    hiring freezes, 46–47, 48
    importance to success, 12
    layoffs, 252
    leasing, 115, 169–170
    part-time, 169
    pay cuts, 54–56
    retaining, 19, 166–168
    selling business to, 227–228
    sharing optimism with, 148–149
    training, 171–172
Employment contracts, 238
Employment costs, reviewing, 115
Entertaining, 116
Entrepreneurs, strengths and weaknesses of, 155–156
Equipment
    causing debt problems, 121
    failures as danger sign, 11–12
    leases, 173, 177–178
    protecting from liquidation, 146–147
    as security for loans, 122
    selling excess, 191–192
Example, leadership by, 22
Excess inventory and equipment, liquidating, 35–36, 190–192
Expansion, wrong reasons to seek, 44, 45
Expenses. *See* Cost cutting
Experience, advantage for attorneys, 142–143
Extensions on loans, 261

F

Fads, 210
Family
    borrowing from, 69
    communications with, 78–79
    succession plans for, 223–228, 254–255

Federal government, alliances with, 217
Financial analysis
    determining corrections, 95–96
    key indicators, 85
    main elements, 86–92
    potential problem areas, 92–95
Financial management
    budgets, 198–200
    discomfort with, 4
    importance, 4–5
    before selling business, 235
Financial reports, improving before sales, 235
Financial structure, accountant's review, 62–63
Fixed costs. *See* Overhead costs
Flat growth, 10–11
Free legal advice, 81
Friends
    as advisors, 68–69
    borrowing from, 69
    communications with, 79–80

G

Geographic expansion, as merger benefit, 231
Goals. *See also* Recovery plans
    for cost cuts, 51–53, 123
    manageability of, 163–164
    for recovery plans, 98–99, 147–148
    renewing focus on, 22–23
Graphics technology, 194–195
Grocery stores, 187
Gross profit margin
    in breakeven calculations, 91–92
    industry averages versus, 93–94
    setting targets, 126–127
Growth. *See also* Marketing plans
    costs of, 110–111
    examining potential, 92–93, 108–109, 208–209
    importance of marketing for, 104–105
    profitability versus, 130
    stagnation as danger sign, 10–11

H

Hidden costs, 126
Hiring freezes, 46–47, 48
Hiring new employees, 170–171
Holding companies, 230–231

I

Implementation, seeking help with, 156–157
Impulsive decisions, avoiding, 42–43
Income statements, 235
Indirect costs. *See* Overhead costs
Individual debt adjustment, 246
Industry averages, gross margins, 93–94
Insolvent businesses, selling, 141
Installation, subcontracting, 189
Insurance agents, 66, 250
Insurance costs, 250–251
Intangible assets, 192–193
Interest rates, reviewing on loans and leases, 122
Internal Revenue Service (IRS), late payment penalties, 33
Internet, 150, 211
Interviewing prospective consultants, 160–161
Inventory
    costs of not selling, 126
    as loan security, 123
    liquidating old, 190–192
    protecting from liquidation, 146–147
    selling excess, 190–191
    selling to raise cash, 35–36
Involuntary bankruptcy, 76, 77

J

Jagger, Mick, 217
Job descriptions, 202–203
Jobs, combining, 54–56
Jointly owned assets, 132
Joint product development, 216–217
Joint sales and marketing, 214–215
Joint ventures, 215–216. *See* Strategic alliances

K

Key employees
    as advisors, 67–68
    retaining, 167–168
King Electric case study, 247–255

L

Labor-saving devices, 15
Landlords, 57, 175–176
Large orders, 31, 78
Lawsuits, hiring attorneys for protection against, 64
Lawyers. *See* Attorneys
Layoffs, 252
Leadership
    importance to succession plans, 223–224
    for positive change, 21–23
Leaseback arrangements, 176–177
Lease-purchase agreements, 177
Leases, renegotiating, 173–176, 177–178
Leasing employees, 115, 169–170
Legal actions for debts, 18
Legal fees, 136, 137
Legal restrictions on overhead costs, 119
Letters to customers, 78
Letters to suppliers, 77
Liabilities, assets versus, 17
Line-by-line analysis
    overhead costs, 114–115
    in year-to-year financial comparisons, 90–91
Lines of credit, 34–35
Liquidation
    in Chapter 7 bankruptcy, 136–137, 244
    filing plans for, 137–138
    net value, 139
    old inventory and equipment, 35–36, 190–192, 249
Liquidity, examining, 17
Loans
    consolidating, 63
    from friends, 69
    personal liability, 257, 265
    renegotiating, 179–181
    reviewing, 120–123
Logo changes, 194–195
Losses, prolonging, 46
Loss leaders, 187

M

Machinery. *See* Equipment
Major customers, failures as danger sign, 14
Management change stage, 267–268
Managerial talent, importance to succession plans, 225
Managers, overhead cost review by, 117–118
Marketing alliances, 214–215
Marketing plans
    advertising methods, 109–110
    basic elements, 105–106
    customer data, 106–109
    positive image, 111
    profitability and, 187–188
    setting costs, 110–111
Markets
    examining, 17, 92–93, 108–109
    predicting future, 210
Market surveys, 108
MBA students as consultants, 157–158
Mergers
    overview of procedure, 233–239
    potential benefits, 231–233
    types, 230–231
Merge/sale, 231
Minority ownership, 227–228
Morale, 12, 22–23

N

Name changes, 194
National Technology Transfer Center, 217
Negotiating repayments, 75, 179–181
Negotiating sale of company, 236–237
Net liquidation value, 139
Net worth, improving, 235
New business
    continuing to develop, 150–151
    costs of, 110–111
    how to attract, 109–110
    potential for, 92–93, 108–109
    right reasons to seek, 44–45
New employees, hiring and training, 170–172
New technology, as potential danger sign, 14–15
Noncompete agreements, 140–141

Nunnally, Tom, 259–260

O

Old inventory and equipment, liquidating, 35–36, 190–192
Online sales, 150
Operating agreements for strategic alliances, 220
Optimism, 146, 148–149
Orders, down payments on, 31, 78
Organizational charts, 200–201
Outside consultants. *See* Consultants
Outsourcing, 168–169
Overhead costs
    administrative, 54, 114–115, 117
    avoiding fault-finding for, 118–119
    comparing with revenues, 94–95
    debt, 120–123
    failure to control, 250–251
    importance to profitability, 7–8
    involving managers in review, 117–118
    legal requirements, 119
    line-by-line review, 114–115
    planning approach to, 123
    productivity increases and, 119–120
    sales expenses, 115–117
Owners
    job descriptions for, 202–203
    strengths and weaknesses of, 155–156
    succession plans for, 223–228, 254–255

P

Partial payment of bills, 75
Partnerships. *See* Alliances
Part-time workers, 169
Payables, renegotiating or slowing, 32–33. *See also* Debt; Renegotiating payables
Pay cuts, 54–56
Payment terms
    renegotiating, 32
    for sale of business, 238–239
Peachtree Accounting, 6
Peers as advisors, 68–69
Penalties
    for contract violations, 119
    for overdue taxes, 13, 14, 33

Percentages
    converting costs to, 88–89, 100
    cost of sales, 116–117
Personal assets, protected, 132
Personal finances, adjusting, 37–40, 58
Personal liability
    for business loans, 257, 265
    for overdue taxes, 13
Planning
    to deal with overhead, 123
    for potential exit from business, 141–142
    seeking help with, 156–157
Plans. See Marketing plans; Recovery plans; Succession plans
Positive explanations, 47–49
Positive image, 111
Prepayments on large orders, 31, 78
Pricing
    basic considerations, 7
    of companies, 234
    compared to industry averages, 93–94
    consulting services, 164
    effects of technology on, 14–15
    increases, 62
    as indication of target market, 126
    major considerations, 126–130
Priority setting, 99–100, 156
Priority tax claims, 136–137
Private consultants. See Consultants
Product benefits, discovering, 107–108
Product development, joint ventures, 216–217
Product differentiation, influence on pricing, 127–128
Productivity, 11–12, 119–120
Products and services
    analyzing profitability, 184–187
    refocusing, 125, 252–253
    selling unprofitable lines, 189–190, 193–194
Professional advisors
    bringing together, 65–66
    candidates for, 61–62, 65–66
    need for, 60–61
Profitability
    analyzing, 184–187

cash flow versus, 28
main elements, 7, 86–92
as marketing goal, 187–188
measures to improve, 183, 188–195, 252–253
of new customers, 110–111
overall strategy, 184
productivity and, 119–120
sales volume versus, 85, 88, 91–94, 130, 188, 208–209
setting gross targets, 126–127, 209
Profit margin, 91–92
Progress reviews, 102–103
Projecting cash flows, 52
Project reviews, 71, 250
Public agencies, consultants from, 158–159
Purchasing power, combined, 232

Q
QuickBooks, 6
Quick fixes, avoiding, 42

R
Real estate, selling, 176–177
Receivables
    diligent collections, 29–30
    as loan security, 123
Record keeping, 4–5
Recovery plans
    goal setting, 98–99, 147–148
    reviewing progress, 102–103
    setting priorities, 99–100
    task lists, 101–102
    timetables, 100–101
Reference checking, 162, 172
Renegotiating payables
    debt, 75, 179–181
    to increase cash flow, 32–33
    leases, 173–176, 177–178
    vendor credit, 181
Rent, 57, 114
Reorganization, 135–136, 245
Responsibility
    delegating, 200–201
    passing to next generation, 223–228

Restaurants
    cash flow, 28
    changing target market, 125
    expanding for wrong reasons, 45
    menu price increases, 62
Résumés, 171
Retail business direct costs, 7
Retainage, 248
Retention, 166–168
Retention bonuses, 166, 167
Revenues
    gross margins versus, 91–92, 93–94
    major costs versus, 86–92
    overhead versus, 94–95
    sales declines, 92–93
    stagnating growth as danger sign, 10–11
Robert Morris Associates, 93

S

Sacred cows, 53–54
Sales
    alliances for, 214–215
    budgeting, 198–199
    of companies, 140–141, 229, 233–239
    continuing to develop, 150–151
    cost analysis, 186
    examining growth potential, 92–93, 108–109, 208–209
    importance of analyzing declines, 87–92, 93
    of real estate, 176–177
    relation to prices, 128–129
    reviewing expenses, 115–117
    right reasons to increase, 44–45
    of unprofitable lines, 189–190
    volume declines, 92–93
    volume versus profitability, 85, 88, 91–94, 130, 188
Sales tax theft, 13
Saviors, 47
Scope of improvement goals, 163–164
SCORE (Service Corps of Retired Employees), 158–159
Season tickets, 193
Second bank accounts, 34–35

Security
    for loans, 122–123, 257, 262, 265
    for vendor credit, 181
September 11 attacks, effect on airlines, 50, 74
Service businesses, direct costs, 7
Service calls, cost analysis, 185
Service Corps of Retired Executives (SCORE), 158–159
Shared promotions, 214–215
Shared resources, 216
Sidewalk sales, 191
Signs of trouble, seven, 10–15
Sleep disturbances, 78–79
Slowing payables, 32–33
Small Business Administration, 158-159
Small Business Development Centers, 66, 158
Software, 86
Solvency, 17, 138–141
Stagnating revenues, 10–11
Stand-still agreements, 259
Statements of outstanding balance, 30
Strategic alliances
    contracts and agreements, 218–221
    examples, 213
    joint product development, 216–217
    in King Electric case study, 253–254
    reasons to create, 211, 214–216
    seeking partners and advice, 217–219
Strategy development, 156
Students as consultants, 157–158
Subcontractors, 168–169, 188–189
Succession plans
    basic requirements, 223–225
    importance, 223
    in King Electric case study, 254–255
    to unrelated parties, 227–228
    written agreements, 225–227
Suppliers, letters to, 77
Support teams. *See* Professional advisors
Surveys, 108

T

Target markets, changing, 125, 252–253

Taxes
   claims in Chapter 7 bankruptcy, 136–137
   as consideration in succession plans, 225–226
   forced collection, 135
   misuse of, 257, 264–265
   unpaid, 13–14, 18–19, 33
Team spirit, 74
Technical assistance programs, 159
Technology
   monitoring trends in, 150, 209–210
   as potential danger sign, 14–15
   sharing as merger benefit, 232
Telephone cost savings, 251
Temporary employment firms, 169
Termination fees, 178
Terminology of accounting, 7–8
Timetables, 100–101, 164
Trade-ins, 192
Training, 171–172
Transaction costs, 117
Travel industry changes, 211
Trends, 10–15, 149–150
Trouble, degrees of, 16
Trustees, 137, 244
Turnaround consultants. *See* Consultants
Turnaround plans. *See* Recovery plans
TWA Airlines, 12

U

United Airlines, 194
Universities, consultants from, 157–158
Unpaid taxes. *See* Taxes
Unsecured debt payments, 135–136, 137
US Airways, 167

V

Value, net liquidation, 139
Variable costs, 7, 126

Vendors
   communications with, 74–77
   cooperation with cost cuts, 56–57
   credit status with, 18
   renegotiating debt with, 135–136, 181
   sharing optimism with, 148–149
Virtual corporations, 217
Vision, renewing focus on, 22–23

W

Wages and salaries
   continual increases, 10
   cutting costs for, 54–56, 250
   as percentage of costs, 89
Web sites
   National Technology Transfer Center, 217
   SCORE, 158
   for selling old inventory and equipment, 36
   Small Business Administration, 159
   Small Business Development Center (SBDC), 66
Wilke, David M., 262
Wisman, Patrick, 267
Withholding taxes, failure to pay, 257, 260, 264–265
Working arrangements with consultants, 162–165
Working capital reserves, 210–211, 261
Workload, reassessing, 46–47
Workout departments, 180, 260–261
World Trade Center attacks, effect on airlines, 50, 74
World Wide Web, 150, 211

Y

Year-to-year financial comparisons, 86–90

Start-Up Guides
Books
Software

To order our catalog call 800-421-2300.
Or visit us online at smallbizbooks.com

Entrepreneur Magazine's
SmallBizBooks.com